Canyoneering 2

Canyoneering 2

Technical Loop Hikes
in Southern Utah

Steve Allen
Foreword by Harvey Halpern

University of Utah Press
Salt Lake City

The Defiance House Man colophon is a registered trademark
of the University of Utah Press. It is based upon a four-foot-tall,
Ancient Puebloan pictograph (late PIII) near Glen Canyon, Utah.

Interior book design by Scott Engen/Booksmith, Salt Lake City, Utah

∞Printed on acid-free paper

Library of Congress Cataloging-in-Publication Data
Allen, Steve, 1951–
    Canyoneering 2 : technical loop hikes in southern Utah / Steve
Allen : foreword by Harvey Halpern.
        p.   cm.
    Includes bibliographical references (p.).
    ISBN 978-0-87480-467-6 (acid-free paper)
    1. Hiking—Utah—Guidebooks. 2. Rock climbing—Utah—Guidebooks.
3. Utah—Guidebooks. I. Title. II. Title: Canyoneering two.
GV199.42.U8A55   1995
796.5'1'09792—dc20   94-31739

Contents

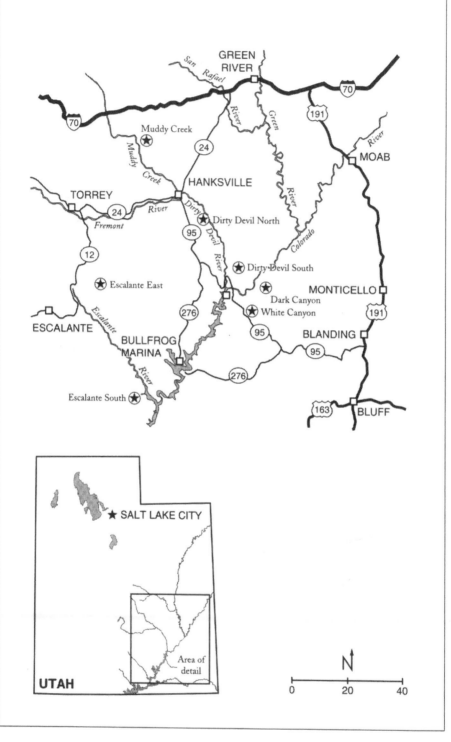

About This Book

Canyoneering 2: Technical Loop Hikes is not for everyone! The guide is designed for experienced desert hikers who are used to covering long distances over rough terrain. All of the routes present a variety of problems, and most require the use of technical rock-climbing equipment for ascending steep rock walls or rappeling down sheer cliffs. At least one person in every group must be proficient at rope work and must have had extensive training on difficult rock faces. A couple of days in a rock-climbing class does *not* qualify you to attempt most of the routes in this guide.

Several of the routes entail hiking long stretches between water sources. This may require carrying two or more gallons of water in packs that are already heavy. It is essential that everyone in your group be in excellent physical condition before heading into the backcountry. Long, hard, hot days are the norm, not the exception. A knowledge of both the prevention and the treatment of hyperthermia is crucial.

Most of the hiking is cross-country; there are few trails. You must be proficient at reading maps. Finding the correct route into a canyon may mean the difference between reaching a water source or finding yourself in dire straits.

If you have any doubts about your qualifications to do any of the routes, they are not for you. Those with enough miles under their feet and days under the rim know who they are. Even hikers with extensive experience must be willing to turn back if things don't go as planned. None of the routes is worth injury—or worse.

Medical evacuation, Waterpocket Fold.

Most of the activities described in *Canyoneering 2: Technical Loop Hikes* carry a significant risk. No guide, including this one, can describe the real, changing world and each person's reaction to it. The author and the publisher do not recommend that people attempt any of these routes unless they are qualified, are knowledgeable about the risks involved, and are willing to assume all responsibilities associated with those risks.

Foreword

"This is the most beautiful canyon in all of Canyon-dom!" That is a phrase I have heard Steve Allen utter frequently. After hiking with Steve for many years, I have learned that the canyon we are in at the moment is the one that he thinks is "the best." It isn't that he has forgotten the others, it is that he sees something amazing everywhere he goes. In Twin Corral Box it was a 150-foot pinnacle with a vertical crack running straight up its sheer east face that brought a glint to Steve's eyes. As we wandered by I knew Steve was piecing together a route up that crack, working the moves to the summit in his mind.

On top of The Block, a huge mesa standing high above Dirty Devil country, we had to hike across a series of narrow ridges with steep cliffs dropping off on either side. The exposure was intense and the views magnificent. Steve was alive and animated, grinning from ear to ear as we cautiously proceeded. Not surprisingly, he commented that this was the best: "The best views and the best ridge walk in canyon country."

In Gravel Canyon a pour-off above an imposing stretch of narrows brought us to a halt. As we pulled ropes out of our packs, Steve laid out the ground rules. We would follow the basic canyoneering axiom that you must always leave yourself a way out. This meant leaving a rope at every drop so that we could climb back up if the route could not be continued. Steve's second rule was that we only use natural protection to anchor our ropes. If bolts were needed, then the canyon would not be doable by "fair means." We would leave the canyon to others more skilled than ourselves. Our fun would not come at the expense of the environment. We were able to complete our descent of the narrows of Gravel Canyon. It took several rappels, a long stretch of chimneying high above the floor of the canyon, a swim or two, and a couple of difficult climbing moves. This awesome canyon was yet another "best ever" canyon for Steve.

For twenty-five years Steve has been exploring the canyons of southern Utah. I believe he knows more about those canyons than any other person. Steve has brought to the canyons the techniques he learned as a rock climber, mountaineer, and guide. While other guidebooks might lead you up and back down the same canyon, Steve will take you to the end of a canyon, up a devious slot or along an impossible-looking ledge, over a bench that affords spectacular views, and then down some little chimney into a wild slot where you can touch both walls at once while the sky peeks in from hundreds of feet above.

Every hike described in *Canyoneering 2: Technical Loop Hikes* contains what Steve believes are the four essential elements of every great canyoneering route: spectacular canyons, intimate narrows, big views, and physical challenge. The routes are not obvious; that's why we are indebted to Steve for writing this book. He has taken the time to explore dead end after dead end until he has found a route that will "go"—and one that will delight the hiker every inch of the way. Most of Steve's routes are so unlikely that it is hard to conceive how he could have put them together. In fact, a week-long route takes Steve many months of exploring to get it right. A long loop may have been first explored in midwinter with sixteen days worth of food in his 100-pound pack. After that, Steve will return two or three more times to scope out each day's journey so that you and I can actually complete the trip.

In Stevens Canyon I had a good chance to observe how Steve works. He knew that there was an easy route out of the middle portion of the canyon—the Baker Trail—but he was interested in finding a way out at the head of the canyon near the top of the Waterpocket Fold. Stevens Canyon in its upper recesses seems to be ringed by unclimbable Wingate cliffs. With a determination bordering on obsession, we spent several days exploring every niche, crack, ledge system, and chimney in the sheer cliffs. During that time we found a half-dozen exits—most were insanely difficult. Steve was looking for a route where the less experienced would not be endangered. Our group would sit at the bottom of the cliffs watching as Steve made his way upwards. One near-vertical chimney ended high atop a ledge system that Steve said was within ten feet of being possible. Another route along a thin ledge above an overhang was feasible but not practical. A third route followed a row of worn Moqui steps up a crease in the canyon wall, but there was too much exposure. The final route we tried, the one presented in the Escalante South chapter, was reasonable and the right one for this book. This testing procedure showed Steve at his best.

It is only because of Steve's major commitment of time that a book like this or his previous book, *Canyoneering: The San Rafael Swell*, could be written. But it takes more than time: it takes a willingness to hike alone in the cold of winter or the heat of summer; it takes an experienced eye and a tremendous amount of skill to determine which routes will go and which are too dangerous; and it takes stubborn devotion and determination to hike every side canyon and to explore every potential route. Of more importance, Steve's love of this precious yet fragile wonderland of southern Utah is what made this book possible. It is his recognition that each and every one of the unique areas presented in this guide is threatened—some by rampant off-road vehicle use, some by new and unneeded roads, some by dams, some by mining, and most by a combination of these things—that pushed him to share this landscape with us. This book opens up new territory to even the most seasoned canyoneer. When you hike in these areas, you should be aware that unless each one of us takes up the challenge of protecting these lands as Wilderness, we can and will lose them for all time.

Harvey Halpern

Acknowledgments

The staff of the University of Utah Press supplied essential support. Their input was invaluable at every twist and turn. Sincere thanks to Rodger Reynolds and Jeff Grathwohl.

More than a hundred backpackers spent time with me in the backcountry while I was preparing this guide. Most of them offered criticism and advice. I extend a special thanks to those who joined me on more than one adventure—your patience was astounding; I can think of many times when, near the end of a long hard day, my companions waited patiently while I took a quick look up a side canyon or backtracked for a mile to make sure I had the description right. The following canyoneers were especially helpful: Ace Allen, Joe Breddan, Larry Breed, Glen Buelteman, Ronnie Egan, Clem Engle, Bud Evans, Jim Finch, Bert and Caroline Fingerhut, Karen Halgren, Rob May, Barbara Moore, Don Murch, Marcey Olajos, Jonathan Rapp, Rob Roseen, and Laverne Waddington.

Wendy Chase hiked most of the routes with me, helped edit the manuscript, designed the geology cross-section charts, and was otherwise essential in preparing the guide for publication. A thousand thanks.

Ginger Harmon hiked all of the routes with me, boosted my spirits when the times were tough, helped edit the manuscript, and encouraged me every step of the way. A special thanks.

Bill and Lyn Booker opened their home to me and shared their love of the canyons.

Ann Perius-Parker joined me in the backcountry and prepared all of the photographs for publication. Thanks, Red.

Harvey Halpern hiked most of the routes with me, was always willing to proof the manuscript during its many stages, and was kind enough to provide many of the photographs for the guide.

Bob Bordasch joined me on many backcountry excursions, helped edit the manuscript, and was always patient while assisting with the map work.

Tom Messenger joined me several times in the backcountry and offered advice on the geologic aspects of the guide.

Utah Place Names by John W. Van Cott was an indispensable reference. Van Cott's careful documentation of the derivation of toponyms in Utah makes his book essential reading for all canyon country enthusiasts.

Several people were not able to join me on the hikes but were, nonetheless, essential. A heartfelt thanks to Mike Sutak, Tom Weinreich, Rick and Beverly Upham, and the proprietors of Escalante Outfitters, Barry and Celeste Bernards.

Introduction

*The shadows of foliage, the drift of clouds, the fall of rain upon
leaves, the sound of running waters—all the gentler qualities
of nature that minor poets love to juggle with—are missing on
the desert. It is stern, harsh, and at first repellent. But what
tongue shall tell the majesty of it, the eternal strength of it, the
poetry of its wide-spread chaos, the sublimity of its lonely desola-
tion. And who shall paint the splendor of its light; and from
the rising up of the sun to the going down of the moon over the
iron mountains, the glory of its wondrous coloring! It is a
gaunt land of splintered peaks, torn valleys, and hot skies.*

John C. Van Dyke, 1901

In September 1861 a Mormon newspaper described
southern Utah as "one vast 'contiguity of waste' and meas-
urably valueless, except for nomadic purposes, hunting
grounds for Indians, and to hold the world together."
Since those words were written southern Utah has become increasingly popular. In years past, writers and photographers flocked to canyon country and painted a
mesmeric picture, the golden glow on a Wingate wall at
sunset, a hidden alcove framed by the green of maidenhair
ferns and the red of monkey flowers, the burbling of a
stream as it wound a sinuous course down a tortuous defile. Hikers, captivated by the images, have come to the
canyons in droves, intent on experiencing the magnificence and mystery only such an area can offer. For the cas-
ual hiker, there is an abundance of material available to
help map out routes and plan adventures. But for the
hard-core canyoneer, there is a dearth of information.

The purpose of *Canyoneering 2: Technical Loop Hikes*
is to help close that gap. This guide describes seven long
backpack trips into some of the most unspoiled and least-
visited areas on the Colorado Plateau. The hikes take one
far from the mainstream into an unexpected world of intense beauty and physical challenge. *Canyoneering 2: Technical Loop Hikes* is not solely for the seasoned backpacker:
although the routes delineated are difficult, the newcomer
to the canyons will find a wealth of information in the
guide that can be used to plan less intimidating excursions.

All of the hikes in the guide are designed as loops. This negates the need for tedious, time-consuming, and gas-wasting car shuttles. One of the aggravating aspects of hiking in southern Utah is finding the trailhead. The miles of old mining roads and stock access tracks in the area can confuse even the veteran canyoneer. Detailed road sections in the book will help ensure that time is not squandered trying to find a trailhead.

Each hike is prefaced with a brief description of the route. This includes details regarding trip length, elevation range, maps, recommended hiking seasons, skill level needed, and special equipment required. The route descriptions contain information on the availability of water, hiking time between known landmarks, descriptions of side trips, and interesting route variations. Maps are included that show important water sources and routes in and out of canyon systems.

The canyons of southern Utah are up for grabs. Mining, ranching, and energy interests are endeavoring to keep the canyons from being protected by wilderness designation. The recent influx of backcountry users also has led to the unintentional degradation of some of the popular canyons. The chapters on "Wilderness" and "Protecting the Environment" discuss these problems.

Some backcountry enthusiasts have a dim view of guidebooks, feeling that they take the adventure out of visiting new areas. For those few, the guidebook should remain on the shelf unused. The thrill of exploration can remain intact. Most backpackers, however, have only a week or two a year to devote to the canyons. Many have to plan their trips far in advance and away from their remote destinations. They are not in a position to get the "beta" from the locals. Unable to spend the time necessary to search out new routes, and unwilling to squander a hard-earned vacation exploring the prosaic in an effort to find the pristine, they tend to flock to the places that they know will provide them with a gratifying experience. Unfortunately, the list of well-known canyons is, at present, short. The result has been serious overcrowding of those canyons on the "tick" list. But, for every Paria Canyon or Coyote Gulch, there are a hundred unnamed and unknown canyons that equal them in resplendence and intensity.

Over the last couple of years the number of deaths and serious injuries in the canyons of southern Utah has increased dramatically. The tragic deaths of two Boy Scout leaders in Zion National Park and two major rescues in the Black Hole of White Canyon in 1993, and the scores of rescue operations in the Upper Black Box of the San Rafael River over the last two years have underscored the need for reliable information. This guidebook does describe country that is unknown to most people. It is my belief that by offering alternatives to the popular canyons, stressing the importance of wilderness advocacy, and harping on the need for low-impact camping techniques, *Canyoneering 2: Technical Loop Hikes* will help spread the visitation load and mitigate the impacts on the land.

The reader may wonder how the routes were chosen. I spent an extensive amount of time in each area: sixteen months in the San Rafael Swell, eight months in the Dirty Devil, four months in White Canyon, three months in Dark Canyon, and close to two years in the Escalante. During that time I found what I considered to be the most beautiful and intriguing places in each area. I then located water sources and found routes in and out of the canyons and across the benchlands in between.

With a wealth of information on each area, I sat down with maps and notes and put together routes that were both interesting and perhaps a bit removed from the norm. I hiked each of the proposed routes in at least two seasons to see if they were viable. Friends joined me on these trips and their comments were invaluable. Short trips were used to double-check water sources and to scout route variations. Only then did I deem the routes acceptable. I have led Sierra Club, Four Corners School, university, and/or private trips on every route—some many times. I think you will find the information in *Canyoneering 2: Technical Loop Hikes* to be helpful and accurate.

Those with less experience hiking in the canyons should start with the easier and less technical routes. The lists below rate the difficulty of the routes, both physically and technically, from easiest to hardest.

Physical challenge:

1. Escalante East
2. White Canyon
3. The Dirty Devil North
4. Muddy Creek
5. Escalante South
6. Dark Canyon
7. The Dirty Devil South

Technical difficulty:

1. Muddy Creek
2. Escalante East
3. The Dirty Devil North
4. The Dirty Devil South
5. Escalante South
6. Dark Canyon
7. White Canyon

Wilderness

We preserve paintings, we preserve our masterpieces of music and art and literature. We treasure them. We build great buildings to protect them. We should at the same time treasure wilderness because wilderness has the same impact on the human mind and spirit. It has the finest emanations of culture which the mind of man has conceived.

Sigurd F. Olson, 1961

It has been more than thirty-five years since I first slung on a backpack and headed into the wilds of Washington's Olympic Peninsula. The thing I remember most about that trip was my huge pack that, in reality, contained only a large dacron sleeping bag. My father carried a truly immense load consisting of all the equipment my twin brother Ace and I were not able to carry. I don't recall the hiking portion of the trip, but I do remember camping by a lake surrounded by the smooth walls of a cirque. After a chilly night, we awoke to an ethereal mist hanging over the water. As the sun warmed the land and the mist rose, we watched mountain goats playing on the cliffs. Ace and I were six or seven.

Since that first hike, our family has explored most of the High Sierra, the coastal ranges of California, and the island ranges of Nevada. Most family hiking time has been spent in the desert regions of the West: the Columbia River Gorge in Washington State, the Sheldon Antelope Range, Black Rock Desert, and Pyramid Lake areas of Nevada, and the Mojave and Sonoran deserts of southern California, Arizona, and northern Mexico. Our last long hike as a family was an extended sojourn into the Ruby Mountains of Nevada a couple of years ago. My mother, at seventy-something, had a bit of trouble with an aching hip and declared that it was her last backpack trip. We'll see.

After I moved to Colorado in 1969, friends introduced me to the canyons of Utah. For twenty years I practically commuted back and forth between Fort Collins and canyon country, often making the drive for only a day or two of exploring. I finally came to my senses and moved to Hanksville, Utah. For the past six years I have spent most of my time backpacking in the canyons of the Colorado Plateau.

Over the years I have witnessed the slow diminishment of our wildlands. Rarely has it been the wholesale degradation of an area; rather, it has been the nibbling around the edges: a new road here, a new stock tank or corral there, a gravel quarry, a timber cut, or the introduction of off-road vehicles or cattle into otherwise pristine areas. Unfortunately, the chomping hasn't stopped and the piece of wilderness pie remaining keeps getting smaller.

Two hundred years ago nearly all of the lands in the United States were wilderness; now only eight percent remains in natural condition. In an effort to save our vanishing wilderness, Congress passed the Wilderness Act in 1964. That act defined wilderness as "an area where the earth and its community of life are untrammeled by man, where man himself is a visitor who does not remain." The Wilderness Act further stated that wilderness is an area where one can find solitude and where there is the opportunity for primitive and unconfined recreation. Unfortunately the Wilderness Act only applied to certain U.S. Forest Service, National Park Service, and Fish and Wildlife Service lands.

In 1976 Congress enacted the Federal Lands Policy Management Act (FLPMA). It applied to lands controlled by the Bureau of Land Management (BLM). FLPMA required that the BLM inventory its holdings to see which lands were suitable for wilderness designation. The BLM was to use the definition of wilderness provided in the Wilderness Act. Once the BLM had determined which lands met the criterion for wilderness, Congress then would decide their final disposition. FLPMA asserted as well that outdoor recreation could be considered a principal or major use of public lands. This was far different from the traditional multiple-use concept of BLM lands.

By 1980 the BLM in Utah had done a cursory inventory of its 22 million acres and had found that 3.2 million of those acres might have wilderness qualities. These acres became Wilderness Study Areas (WSAs). Over the next eleven years the BLM conducted an intensive inventory of the WSAs. By 1991 it found that of the initial 3.2 million acres, only 1.9 million were worthy of wilderness designation.

The BLM wilderness inventory process has come under attack from environmental groups who felt that the BLM did not use the congressional definition of wilderness. They believed that the BLM had declared areas worthy or not worthy of wilderness designation based on the agency's own whims and fancies. They noted that most of the lands excluded from wilderness consideration by the BLM had the potential for economic development—whether that be for mines, dam sites, or stock improvements.

One example of the BLM's wilderness inventory process exemplifies its refusal to follow the congressional mandate in determining which lands should be considered for wilderness designation. A large portion of the Dirty Devil River drainage has been removed from wilderness consideration because it is in the "Tar-sands Triangle." Two problems immediately arise. The first is that the area meets the congressional definition of wilderness and should therefore be a part of the BLM wilderness proposal.

The second problem is tangential, but it is indicative of the faulty and self-serving nature of the BLM's inventory process. The Tar-sands Triangle lands contain up to 1.6 billion barrels of oil, of which half may be economically recoverable. While 800 million barrels seems like a lot of oil, that amount would only supply the nation's needs for about two months. When compared to the 12.5 to 18 billion barrels of oil contained in tar sands that underlie areas in Utah not deemed suitable for wilderness designation, coupled with a national oil-shale reserve of 600 billion barrels of oil, the problem becomes clear. Should we sacrifice for all time a wilderness area that will produce an insignificant amount of oil from a national perspective and whose sacrifice will bring monetary gain to just a few?

The environmental groups decided that Congress needed an accurate description of the wildlands in southern Utah to counter the inaccurate information presented by the BLM. In 1985 they formed the Utah Wilderness Coalition (UWC), an association of thirty-five conserva-

Drill rig above Dark Canyon.

tion groups that includes the Sierra Club, the Wilderness
Society, the National Parks and Conservation Association,
and the Southern Utah Wilderness Alliance. Members of
the UWC logged thousands of hours in the field while doing their own survey. They used the congressional definition of wilderness as a guide. Their research, detailed in
the book *Wilderness at the Edge*, determined that 5.7
million acres of BLM land were worthy of wilderness
designation. These lands are included in the UWC's
5.7-million-acre wilderness proposal, which is the basis for
H.R. 1500, a bill first introduced in Congress in 1989 by
then Utah Representative Wayne Owens.

Critics of this proposal proclaim that too much land
will be tied up with wilderness designation if it is imple-
mented. From a pragmatic viewpoint, I and other environ-
mentalists find that this has little basis in reality. The BLM
controls 22 million acres in Utah, most of it in the southern part of the state. The H.R. 1500 bill would affect only
about a quarter of that land. Traditional uses of the land
would continue. Cattle grazing, for example, is allowed in
wilderness. Mining is permitted if the claims were filed before FLPMA was enacted in 1976. While off-road vehicle
(ORV) users may complain that they won't have a place
to ride, the fact is that they will still have about 17 million
acres of other BLM land to play on—to say nothing about

Anti-wilderness sign, San Rafael Swell.

other federal lands and state lands that are open to ORV use.

Critics must realize that lands preserved as wilderness will not only benefit the hiker and backcountry explorer; wilderness can bring economic activity to nearby depressed communities; provide habitat for both game animals and endangered species; protect valuable watershed resources; safeguard archaeological sites; and promote biological diversity. By preserving wilderness, we are protecting values that may be intangible now but will be critical in the future.

In 1961 Howard Zahniser, the former executive secretary of the Wilderness Society, wrote: "We not only value the wilderness because of its own superlative values but because our experience in the wilderness meets fundamental human needs. These needs are not only recreational and spiritual, but also educational and scientific, not only personal but cultural. They are profound. For the wilderness is essential to us, as human beings, for a true understanding of ourselves, our culture, our own natures, our place in all nature. . . . Primeval wilderness, once gone, is gone forever; but it can be preserved forever."

For an increasing number of people, the quality of their life is dependent on wilderness access. Wilderness provides opportunities to escape the pressures of everyday life, to explore aesthetic and spiritual values, to test one's competence and self-reliance, to learn about nature, and to find tranquility and solitude. As the daily pressures of modern life increase, the need for wilderness also increases.

Those entering the wildlands described in this guide must pay a high price for the privilege, a cost above the discomforts of a heavy pack, tired muscles, blistered feet, or a lack of water. Those who relish the hardships afforded by the canyons and revel in their magnificence must become advocates for the preservation of wilderness. The Southern Utah Wilderness Alliance (SUWA) is the most active and effective organization dedicated to saving the lands covered in this guide. It has been instrumental in keeping the excesses of the federal land agencies in check. Please make it a habit to donate to SUWA after every adventure; consider it a part of the cost of enjoying the canyons of southern Utah.

Southern Utah Wilderness Alliance
1471 South 1100 East
Salt Lake City, Utah 84105-423
801-486-3161

Protecting the Environment

*This is our land, the beauty and majesty of which must be pre-
served not only for ourselves but for the enjoyment and inspira-
tion which future generations in a more crowded world will
have a need even more urgent than we of today.*
Randall Henderson, 1968

In the early 1960s my idea of good camping technique was to throw my cans in the fire, let the zinc coat-
ing burn off, then bury them a foot underground. My
repertoire also included building lean-tos from freshly cut
pine boughs and digging carefully engineered trenches
around the old canvas tent. The scars left on the landscape
were manifold, but there were only a few crazy people out
hiking and their impact seemed insignificant. The times
have changed. Thirty years ago a popular canyon was one
that was visited by a half-dozen people a year; the number
now may be in the thousands. And the land is taking a
beating.

The solution is not easy. The meticulous use of mini-
mum-impact camping techniques can help spare the land;
but this is no longer enough. We must now become our
brother's keeper. It is our responsibility to clean up any
mess left by others. Leave room in your pack for extra garbage. Even those old cowboy camp dump sites will slowly
disappear if each person carries out one can or bottle.
Spend ten minutes breaking up an old fire ring, blocking
off a redundant trail, or restoring an ill-used campsite. In-
sensitive hikers can no longer be tolerated. It is our obliga-
tion to help educate those who don't know and to
chastise those who do know but don't care.

Please read the following section carefully.

Trash: The most obvious eyesore. Take out more than
you bring in.

Bodily waste: Solid waste should be disposed of at least
300 feet from any water source. Dig a hole six to eight
inches deep near vegetation and with maximum exposure

to sunlight. The microorganisms associated with the vegetation as well as the heat available from the sun will speed the breakdown of the waste. In the popular canyons it is no longer sufficient to burn your toilet paper; you must carry it out. Plastic bags make this easy and odor free. Grand Canyon backpackers have been carrying out their toilet paper for years. Urinate on slickrock or in sandy washes. Do not urinate on vegetation.

Camp hygiene: A gray-water hole should be used at every campsite. As with bodily waste areas, this hole should be six to eight inches deep, near vegetation, and with maximum exposure to the sun. Leftover food, the dregs from dishwashing, and toothpaste can all go in the hole. Do not wash dishes in streams or potholes and do not throw leftovers into the bushes. In the popular canyons make it a practice to carry out your leftover food.

Bathing: Water on most of the hikes is scarce and should be treated as a treasured commodity. Pothole water should be used only for cooking and drinking; other groups of backpackers may be depending on the water. Save your swimming and bathing for the creeks and rivers; swim in potholes only if there is a substantial flow of water. If you need to lather up, use pots and canteens to carry water well away from the water source. Use only pure soaps like Dr. Bronner's Castile or Ivory bar soaps. They don't have the perfumes and additives that are damaging to the environment.

Indian artifacts and ruins: The relics left behind by Anasazi and Fremont Indians belong to all of us and are protected by law. Treat the sites as if they were the private property of a friend. It is illegal to remove Indian artifacts or to vandalize any archaeological feature. When visiting ruins, stay on established paths, do not enter the ruins, and do not climb the walls. Do not camp or build fires in or near ruins. Rock art should be viewed from a distance; do not touch it, brush it, or use chalk to outline the figures.

Campsite selection: The area that takes the most abuse

from backpackers is the campsite. For that reason, campsite selection is of primary importance. There are several things to think about when choosing a campsite: (1) Camp at least 200 feet from water sources. When camping near isolated potholes, springs, or ponds, do not use the water source after dark because you may scare away wild animals. (2) Use a well-established site. The damage has already been done. If a site has been lightly used, it is best to find a heavily used site or move on to a new site and let the lightly used site recover. (3) Camp on slickrock or in a dry wash, weather permitting. These are the optimal sites since there are no lasting impacts. (4) Do not camp in areas where microbiotic soil is present. (5) Do not remove vegetation to level or smooth out sleeping platforms. (6) If debris—branches, rocks, leaves—have been cleared to make a campsite, return it to its original location before moving on. Unless the campsite has been heavily used in the past, you should be able to erase all signs of your use.

Fires: Fires can no longer be tolerated in the wilderness setting. They do an immense amount of damage to the land. Not only are the blackened rocks of a fire ring ugly, the charcoal and ash residues seem to last forever. Fire rings also demarcate campsites and tend to draw people to them, which promotes overuse.

Use a lightweight stove for cooking and a candle lantern as a gathering beacon for nighttime socializing. In *The Telling Distance*, author Bruce Berger wrote this about camp fires: "What I really can't stand is the way everyone stares at the coals after dinner without saying anything. The fire is the camper's boob tube."

Microbiotic soil: Also called cryptogamic soil, this is a conglomeration of algae, fungi, moss, and lichen that forms the black, castle-like crust that is found throughout the desert. It is invaluable in holding the soil together and reducing erosion. Stay on established trails when walking through areas of microbiotic soil. If there are no trails, follow your predecessor's footsteps. Do not leave a trail where erosion can start.

Dogs: Dogs are allowed in all of the areas covered in this guide. Be realistic about the quality of your animal. If it is loud, aggressive toward other hikers or wildlife, chases cattle, defecates on the trails, doesn't respond to your commands, or is in other ways obnoxious, leave it behind. In some areas water sources are infrequent and become very valuable. Don't let your dog muddy up an isolated water source. Dog owners should make it a practice to leash their pets when other hikers are nearby.

Cairns: Both a bane and a boon, these short stacks of rocks are erected to mark the trail. Unfortunately, there are too many "cairns to nowhere," and these should be toppled. Some cairns can be an environmental plus—they keep hikers on established paths and reduce the incidence of multiple trails.

Rappel anchors: Several of the routes described in this book require the use of climbing ropes for rappels. When setting up rappels it may seem environmentally preferable to simply wrap the rope around a tree or shrub and not use a sling and rappel rings. However, damage can occur to bark or branches when the ropes are pulled. If enough people do this, the tree or shrub can be injured. The use of webbing and rappel rings can help alleviate the problem. Black or brown sling material reduces its visual impact. Multiple slings are not necessary. Always remove and carry out old slings and do not use someone else's rappel rings.

The use of bolts and other drilled anchors is not appropriate in canyoneering. Part of the challenge of descending technical canyons is using what nature has provided. Drilled anchors are not only visually intrusive but also are rarely placed correctly. Several years ago drilled anchors were installed in the South Fork of Robbers Roost Canyon. When the anchors were recently tested, most of them came out with light pressure from a screwdriver. Considering that hundreds of canyoneers had blithely used these anchors, it is a wonder a serious accident had not occurred.

How to Use This Guide

You will not be surprised then if in speaking of desert, mesa and mountain I once more take you far beyond the wire fence of civilization to those places (unhappily few now) where the trail is unbroken and the mountain peak unblazed.

John C. Van Dyke, 1901

To get the most out of this guide and to help you understand the terminology, read this section carefully. The guide is divided into seven chapters. Each describes a single hike. The route descriptions are prefaced by a concise section that will include the pertinent parameters for that hike. These include:

General description: This consists of an overview of the area, a brief history, and a short description of the route.

Trip length: The number of days suggested for each route applies only to experienced backpackers in good physical condition. If you plan to do lots of exploring, photographing, or relaxing, add extra time to your itinerary. Due to the demanding nature of most of the hikes, it is prudent to carry extra food in case the trip takes longer than planned.

Elevation range: This notes the lowest and the highest elevations on the route.

Recommended seasons: Be aware that recommended dates noted for each hike are only suggestions. Weather extremes in canyon country are the norm. Be prepared to vary your itinerary as the weather dictates. Below are some general guidelines.

February: Winter is starting to wind down by mid-month. Expect temperatures to vary from lows of twenty to highs of seventy degrees Fahrenheit. The last big snows usually arrive during this month and can leave you stranded at the trailhead. There are few other hikers out and about.

March: The first glimmer of spring is tempered by unsettled weather and the chance of snow and rain. Temperatures vary from below freezing to highs of eighty degrees. Trailhead access can be a problem. Spring break ushers in an influx of college students. The canyons start to get busy.

April: Spring is here and the first flowers start to bloom. Rain and high winds are common. Temperatures vary from freezing to ninety degrees. This is the most popular month for backpacking.

May: This is the month that the wind never seems to die down. Plan on temperatures from just above freezing to one hundred degrees by the end of the month. Short rains (snow at higher elevations) are possible. Gnats can be a nuisance as can also be biting flies along watercourses.

June: Summer has fully arrived. Bugs, temperatures over one hundred degrees, and little moisture dictate the end of the hiking season by midmonth.

September: August rains have reinvigorated the desert and the fall bloom has started, but temperatures are still hot, varying from fifty to one hundred degrees. Short rains are possible; however, the weather is usually dry.

October and November: Nighttime temperatures start to drop as the season progresses and the days become shorter. Plan on a gamut of temperature extremes from twenty to ninety degrees. Leaves are changing and the canyons are awash in color. This is my favorite time in the desert. Water is usually plentiful and the crispness of the nights is invigorating.

December: Expect the first of the big snows and nighttime temperatures down to zero degrees. The short days and fourteen-hour nights can be a trial, but you will see few other hikers. Water is rarely a problem, which makes this a good time to explore benchlands and normally dry canyons.

Maps: There are two types of maps listed at the start of each route. The USGS 7.5-minute series topographic maps **must** be carried on all of the hikes. As you move through the text, map changes are indicated by the name of the new map printed in **bold type.**

The metric series maps mentioned are not adequate for hiking but can be helpful for finding the trailheads and for giving a general overview of the area. All of the maps listed are available from:

Escalante Outfitters
310 West Main Street
Escalante, Utah 84726
801-826-4266

The Escalante Outfitters also have most of the 7.5-minute series maps for southern Utah. The cost is the same as from the USGS and they can have the maps to you in a week instead of the couple of months it takes to get them from the USGS.

Two types of maps are used in the guide. The area map at the beginning of each chapter provides a compre-hensive view of the hike and can be helpful in visualizing the route. They are not detailed enough to rely on while in the backcountry.

The most important maps in the guide are based on the 7.5-minute maps and have been reproduced in their original size. Because they have been printed in black and white, the maps do not display features such as areas of vegetation or rivers and creeks in color as they are dis-played on the original USGS maps. The maps in the book show only short stretches of the route and are designed to help locate the harder-to-find canyon exits, entrances, and water sources. It is up to you to fill in the missing pieces, which usually consist of long stretches of straight-ahead hiking where the likelihood of getting lost is reduced. Some may wish to pencil in the whole route on their USGS maps before the start of a trip.

Skill level: Be realistic in assessing your experience, skill, and degree of physical fitness. The routes presented are difficult—physically and mentally. If your group is not as strong as you thought, you could end up in real trouble.

Difficulties in route finding can take several forms. Interpreting the guide and matching it with what you see admittedly can be confusing. Picking your way up or down steep ledges or in and out of canyon systems can be frustrating and time consuming. Note: Keep your map handy and determine where you are at all times. Don't make the mistake of forcing the map and terrain to match when they really don't. These routes are not the place to learn to read a map.

Most of the routes in the guide require the use of climbing ropes and other specialized gear. **Unless you have extensive experience using this equipment, stay away from the technical routes.** Climbing crumbly sandstone in hiking boots is far different from a securely belayed climb at the local crag.

The Yosemite Decimal System is used to describe the roughness of the terrain. This system has been used for years by hikers and climbers throughout the United States. The Yosemite Decimal System is broken down into five classes:

1. Trail or flat walking. No objective dangers.
2. Off-trail walking, some scrambling and boulder hopping. Steeper terrain.
3. Definite scrambling. Hands may be needed for balance. Exposure to heights possible.
4. Large hand- and footholds are used. A fall could have serious consequences. The use of a rope with beginners is often necessary. This is as hard as the average, experienced, and fit hiker can handle. If you get to a section that looks too hard, don't do it. Climbing Class-4 routes with a heavy pack can make them very difficult. Many may wish to use a rope.
5. The fifth-class category, which is normally the start of roped climbing, is broken down into smaller segments, from 5.0 to 5.14. Except for avoidable digressions, there are no problems over Class 5.4 in difficulty in this guide.

If you are not familiar with roped climbing techniques you should stay away from the fifth-class routes. There should be at least one person in your party who can lead the hard parts of a route without protection. Belay anchors and intermediate protection are usually nonexistent. Exposure heights are given in the description of the hikes when applicable. Example: (Class 5.1, 30′) means there is a Class-5.1 move on a thirty-foot-tall wall, slab, or chimney. All ratings assume the use of tennis shoes or hiking boots.

Special equipment: Each hike presents its own set of problems and may require some special equipment. When climbing ropes are mentioned, realize that old clothesline, ski rope, or nylon parachute cord is not adequate. Suitable climbing equipment and a knowledge of how to use it properly are essential.

Several of the routes require short stretches of swimming. Floating packs on a Therm-a-Rest does not work well, nor does stuffing your pack into a large garbage bag—they always seem to snag on something and rip at the wrong time. An automotive-type inner tube does work well and, though heavy, will insure that your pack stays dry. Small bicycle pumps are adequate for inflating the tubes. Hint: Use a valve stem tool to remove the valve from the inner tube. Inflate the inner tube by mouth as much as possible, then use the pump. The tube can be filled quickly this way.

There are several hikes that involve wading. Unless the wading is on smooth sandy terrain, tennis shoes are not adequate. An old pair of lug-soled hiking boots is preferable. Sandals and neoprene booties do not provide adequate support or protection. Hint: Some of the routes require wading just a time or two. It is a cardinal sin to wade barefoot, but for some stream crossings a pair of socks will provide enough protection from sharp edges and also give a good grip.

A compass is essential when using the guide. Don't count on your innate sense of direction to get you through. A couple of sharp turns in a sinuous canyon and you will be confused. Inexpensive compasses work as well as expensive ones.

Road Sections

The road sections direct you to the trailhead for each hike. The introductory paragraph tells you what type of vehicle can make it to the trailhead. Vehicle types are broken down into four categories:

Any vehicle is just that: Winnebagos, Cadillacs, cars towing trailers, etc.

Light-duty vehicles include most small cars: Toyota Corolla, Ford Taurus, Subaru, Nissan, VW Rabbit, etc.

High-clearance vehicles include Volkswagen bugs and buses, short-wheelbase vans, two-wheel-drive pickups, and mini-pickups.

Four-wheel-drive (4WD) roads are for real 4WDs, not for the smaller 4WD cars that don't have the necessary ground clearance.

Rain or snow can make any of the access roads impassable, even to 4WDs. On some roads short sections of deep sand will be encountered. Be aware that roads can change overnight; it is best to be wary. If in doubt, walk through suspect sections of road first. Do not drive any of the roads at night. A black cow on a black road on a black night cannot be seen. Roads that have washed out, sandy sections, deer, and antelope will all conspire against you. Play it safe.

The introductory paragraph informs you whether there is camping at or near the trailhead. This does not mean that there is a campground. It simply means that there are short side roads, washes, or pullouts that can be used for camping. Do not make your own tracks to a campsite. There are enough already. There may be restrictions in some areas; obey all signs.

Next is the mileage list. It starts with a description of where the mileage count starts. All mileage is cumulative. To some, the mileage lists may seem too detailed, but the extra landmarks are meant to reassure. When compass readings are required, be aware that a compass may not point accurately when it is used in a car.

There is a difference between a road and a track. A road, though dirt or gravel, is maintained by occasional grading. Tracks are not maintained and tend to be rougher than roads.

Route Descriptions:

The most important thing to do is to read the route descriptions carefully from beginning to end before your trip. This will help you decide if the route is suitable for your group. Most of the routes are described using a day-to-day format. This is not meant to be confining, and you are encouraged to plan your own itinerary. It is important, however, to be aware of the waterless days that will require you getting from one water source to another.

Time—caveats, cop-outs, and disclaimers: I went day-hiking with a fellow who had complained about the times I had allocated for doing certain routes. He said it took him nearly twice as long as I said it should. The problem became apparent after only a few minutes of walking. Within those minutes, he had scurried to the edge of the canyon, taken a couple of photographs, loaded a new roll of film, zoomed into a side canyon for a look—and we were still in sight of the trailhead. By the end of the day, a very long one at that, he had shot three or four rolls of film and there was nothing in that canyon system of which we weren't aware.

The times mentioned at the beginning of each day mean only one thing: if you hike at a moderate pace, take short breaks, don't dilly-dally around, don't take too many photographs, don't fall asleep after lunch, don't gimp along with horrible blisters, don't die on the uphill, and don't get lost, you should be able to make it to the destination in the stated time. It is always a good idea to allot an extra hour or two per day to cover any exigency that might develop.

The times shown in parentheses ( ) every few paragraphs will help you plan your days and still allow you to determine your own agenda. These times are broad estimates. Do not use them to compute actual hiking time between points.

Water: Water should always be on your mind when hiking in the desert. *Always carry enough water to get back to a known source.* During periods of hot weather start hiking at first light, take a midday break, and resume hiking

in the cool hours of the evening. Human water require-
ments go up in hot weather; two gallons over a twelve-
hour period may be realistic. The prophylactic use of
electrolyte-replacement drinks like ERG and Gatorade is
recommended. Those individuals coming to the area from
cooler climates can take up to ten days to acclimate to the
heat and should take it easy for the first few days. Alcohol
and caffeine are diuretics and promote dehydration. Water
loading, the intake of a quart or two of water before you
start to hike in the morning, works well and can reduce
the amount of water you need to carry on your back.

Water sources, either springs or potholes, are described in the text and on the maps as small, medium, or
large. This does not refer to their physical size but rather
to the likelihood of finding water in them *during the recommended hiking seasons.* These descriptions are subjective
judgments and should not be taken as gospel. Small
means that the water source may dry up within days of a
rain. Medium potholes should hold water for a week or
two after a rain, and a medium spring is one that runs
most of the time but will dry up after long periods without moisture. Large potholes will be full even a month after a rain. Large springs are nearly perennial; they will dry
up only after prolonged drought. Only the large springs
and potholes are generally reliable.

Springs and potholes are shown on the maps and are
described using abbreviations. A large spring or pothole is
marked as **lsg** or **lph**; a medium spring or pothole is
marked as **msg** or **mph**; a small spring or pothole is
marked as **ssg** or **sph**.

*All water should be treated or filtered, without excep-
tion.* Giardia is a hard-shelled protozoan that can cause no
end of bowel distress if you should happen to "get the
bug." The latest medical research has shown that there are
several effective methods for eradicating the pest in your
drinking water.

Heat your water. Giardia, bacteria, and viruses are
killed at a temperature of about 150 degrees. You just
need to bring the water to a boil; you don't have to keep
boiling it.

Use iodine. The two-percent tincture of iodine liquid
available at the grocery store works well. Use five drops

per quart if the water is clear; add five more drops per quart if the water is cloudy. If the water is over 68 degrees Fahrenheit let it sit for thirty minutes before drinking. The colder the water, the longer you need to let it sit. The basic rule when using iodine is to either use a little and let it work for a long period of time or use a lot and wait a shorter period. If you treat the water and then let it sit overnight, you will only have to add one or two drops of iodine per quart. If the taste of iodine-treated water is objectionable, treat the water as prescribed, then take the lid off the water container. The iodine taste will be somewhat lessened. Some people get a sore throat from using iodine.

Iodine tablets such as Potable-Aqua and crystals of iodine (Polar Pure) work well but are expensive. Always use fresh iodine liquid or tablets. Iodine loses its effectiveness when it is exposed to air.

Chlorine and halazone. These compounds are effective against virus and bacteria. They will not kill Giardia, however.

Filters. A good filter can make dirty, scummy, muddy water palatable. The only filter I recommend for desert travel is the Katadyn Pocket Filter. It is initially expensive, but the filter cartridge will last the average hiker a lifetime. The Katadyn is also the only filter on the market that is easy to clean in the field. Hint: Before trying to filter muddy water, first strain it through a disposable coffee filter or let the sediment settle for a couple of hours.

Carrying large quantities of water can be a trial. A Clorox-type bottle wrapped with a layer of duct tape is an inexpensive solution. The MSR Dromedary bags, though costly, are ideal. Light-weight water sacks are not dependable.

Terminology: LDC signifies Looking Downcanyon; LUC means Looking Upcanyon. *Heading* a canyon means walking upcanyon along one rim until it is possible to cross the top of the canyon and walk in the opposite direction along the opposite rim. A *dry camp* is one that is not near water. *Jump-starting* a day is a technique used when a waterless section is ahead. There are variations on the theme, but the idea is to eat dinner near water, then hike for a couple of hours before dark and dry camp. This can substantially reduce the amount of water you need to carry and can help insure that you will get to water the next day.

Within the body of the text there are several features to note. *Options* describe major route variations that can add more time to the hike. The options should be chosen before the start of the trip. *Alternate routes* are short variations that will take you to the same place as the standard route. They are used to describe ways around deep water or to avoid difficult climbing sections. *Digressions* describe short side trips or note points of interest. *Rock-climber's notes* describe short, difficult side trips or route variations that will be of interest to rock climbers. The *Historical notes* try to bring a sense of history to the hikes.

The *Geology lessons* are important. The routes are often described in terms of the rock formations; for example: "Ascend a gully to the top of the Wingate and follow a Kayenta bench downcanyon." The geology lessons are placed either in the road section or near the information on the start of a hike. Familiarize yourself with the formations as you walk along. The geology cross-section charts inside the front and back covers will help. Throughout the manuscript the descriptions of the various formations have been shortened; for example, a Wingate wall instead of a wall of Wingate Sandstone or a Navajo dome instead of a dome of Navajo Sandstone, etc.

The names for features are as historically accurate as possible. Some features are not named on the maps or in the literature but have a local name. When used, these are prefaced by (LKA), Locally Known As. Features which I have named are followed with an (AN)—Author's Name.

The short stories at the start of each chapter not only will introduce you to some of the most respected canyoneers now wandering the deserts of southern Utah but also will give you a sense of the joys—and difficulties—involved in the exploration of the areas covered in the guide. It is, after all, not only the land that we treasure, it is the people with whom we travel that make the journey worthwhile.

Harvey

It was late September and I found myself bouncing along the Reds Canyon loop road toward Muddy Creek. The road starts high on the San Rafael Swell, crosses Sinbad Country, and drops into Reds Canyon, where the road and the canyon floor commingle. The canyon was named for red-bearded "Red" Blackum, and its course is lined with points of interest: Family Butte, with its seven impressive pinnacles, Square Top Butte, Sulphur Spring Canyon, and the Lucky Strike mining area. After rains the road can be difficult to negotiate and, sure enough, as I rounded a corner there was a small car buried up to its axles in wet sand. Two fellows were hard at work with shovels. I parked my van and offered to lend a hand. They introduced themselves as Harvey Halpern and Bud Evans from Cambridge, Massachusetts.

Harvey and Bud were on their way to Muddy Creek to have a go at The Chute, having been told that it was similar to the Narrows of Zion. It was late in the day, therefore, after extracting their rental car from the sand, we camped together below Tomsich Butte. When they learned that I had been down The Chute several times, Harvey asked if I'd like to join them. I accepted their invitation and so began a friendship that has lasted for years.

Harvey was no newcomer to canyon country; his resumé of hikes includes most of the canyons in southern Utah. Harvey unabashedly claims that he has hiked more canyons than anyone living east of the Mississippi. He is probably right. After Harvey's first hike—a five-day trip into the Grand Canyon in 1971—he has made yearly pilgrimages to canyon country, most lasting for two or three months.

Harvey has combined his profound knowledge of the canyons with his talent for photography to further the

Harvey on the Big Ridge above Happy Canyon.

cause of protecting the wildlands of southern Utah. In
conjunction with the Southern Utah Wilderness Alliance,
he has presented his acclaimed slide show to such groups
as the Appalachian Mountain Club, the Massachusetts
Audubon Society, the New England School of Photography, and innumerable hiking clubs and university groups.

The desert trip of which Harvey is most proud was a
sixteen-day rafting expedition down the Dirty Devil River
with a group of friends from Cambridge. The trip turned
into an epic adventure. After losing their sunscreen and
skin lotion when their raft was overturned by high winds
on the first day, they found that the lost potions were
sorely missed—their skin dried and cracked in the heat
and the astringent effect of the muddy river water exacerbated their plight. While the uninitiated might denigrate
their problem, desert rats will nod their heads in sympathy. Dauntlessly continuing on, Harvey's group explored
all of the Dirty Devil's major tributaries and most of its minor ones. Near the end of their voyage, a trio of kayakers
passed them and, seeing their dilapidated condition, reported back to Hanksville that they weren't sure whether
this crazy group from the east would make it out alive.
Hearing this, the proprietors of Tropical Jeems restaurant
in Hanksville sent sandwiches and drinks to the group
with the shuttle driver who was to meet them at the take-

out point near Lake Powell. Although their clothes were in shreds and stained brown from the muddy water, and though their skin was cracked and bleeding, they had completed their remarkable journey.

We had arrived at Muddy Creek just days after a flash flood, so, instead of going down The Chute, we followed the Pasture Track into Chimney Canyon. Harvey was enchanted by the divine, Daliesque-like formations in the upper forks of Chimney Canyon and spent most of his time taking photographs. During our second night in the canyon, the rains came and the canyon flashed. We were awakened by the roar of the fast-moving water and we watched the rising water with a mix of trepidation and delight. The water subsided before it reached our camp; by morning the only evidence left of the flash flood was a wet streambed.

With time running out and unwilling to miss a chance to hike through The Chute, Harvey decided that we should hike up it. On subsequent trips I was to find out that this was a typical Harvey ploy: damn the flash floods, full speed ahead. To Harvey, obstacles are either a nuisance or a source of adventure, but they are never a reason to abandon a trip. I remember that day in The Chute very well. The water in The Chute is rarely more than knee deep, but on this day we found ourselves with packs balanced on our heads, using their weight to hold us down as we waded through chest-deep stretches of water. Harvey's cries of "Watch the cameras!" rang out as we slowly made our way up the canyon and back to the trailhead.

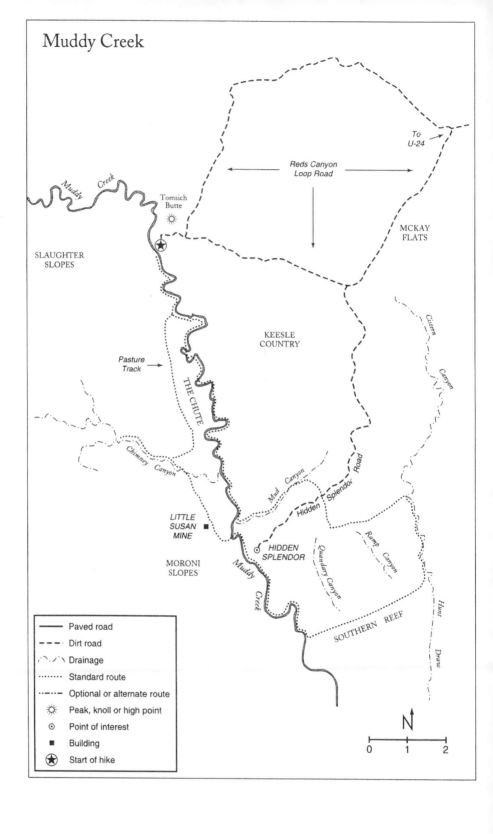

Muddy Creek

Muddy Creek

Tomsich Butte

SLAUGHTER SLOPES

Reds Canyon Loop Road

To U-24

MCKAY FLATS

KEESLE COUNTRY

Cistern Canyon

Pasture Track

THE CHUTE

Chimney Canyon

Mud Canyon

Hidden Splendor Road

LITTLE SUSAN MINE

HIDDEN SPLENDOR

MORONI SLOPES

Muddy Creek

Quandary Canyon

Ramp Canyon

Hunt Draw

SOUTHERN REEF

Paved road
Dirt road
Drainage
Standard route
Optional or alternate route
☀ Peak, knoll or high point
⊙ Point of interest
■ Building
★ Start of hike

N

0 1 2

Muddy Creek in the San Rafael Swell

For all the toll the desert takes of a man it gives compensations, deep breaths, deep sleep, and the communion with stars.
Mary Austin, 1903

General description: Muddy Creek flows for ninety miles, starting in the highlands of the Wasatch Plateau and ending near the small town of Hanksville, where it joins the Fremont River to become the Dirty Devil. During the course of its wanderings, Muddy Creek cuts through the San Rafael Swell—a magnificent area of multicolored badlands, sheer cliffs, and deeply incised canyons. As Muddy Creek skirts the backside of the western reef of the San Rafael Swell, it has cut hundreds of feet into the Coconino Sandstone, leaving behind The Chute, a narrow, sheer-walled canyon similar to the Black Box canyons of the San Rafael River to the north. Other canyons of equal interest are in the vicinity: Mud Canyon is a singular Moenkopi slot; Cistern Canyon in the Southern Reef is an enchanting Navajo-lined narrows; and Chimney Canyon has been called by some the most beautiful in the Swell.

The San Rafael Swell was home to Indians of the Desert Archaic Culture, descendants of the Paleo-Indians who crossed the Bering Sea land bridge some fifteen thousand years ago. The Desert Archaic Indians roamed the San Rafael Swell from 5000 B.C. to A.D. 500. The Fremont Indians arrived from the north around A.D. 500 and had left the area by A.D. 1300. Although extensive evidence of Indian habitation has been found in other areas of the San Rafael Swell, little has been discovered in the Muddy Creek drainage.

In the 1870s the Swaseys, a pioneer Mormon family, moved to the San Rafael Swell. They ran cattle along Muddy Creek and on Sinbad Country, the plateau to the east. The Swasey name is synonymous with the San Rafael Swell: they are responsible for naming many of its features: Sids Leap, Cliff Dweller Flat, Eagle Canyon, Joe and his Dog, and Rods Valley, among many others.

The rush for uranium started in the early 1900s, and ore from Temple Mountain was used by Madame Curie in her studies on the nature of radiation. Uranium from the San Rafael Swell was instrumental in the construction of the first atomic weapons. The uranium miners left behind a legacy of roads, mine workings, and old buildings whose remains can be seen today.

The hike starts at Tomsich Butte and descends The Chute of Muddy Creek. After leaving the main canyon system by way of Mud Canyon, the route crosses a corner of Keesle Country and goes to the Southern Reef. Cistern Canyon is followed south through the reef to its base, a painted desert area with the nearly vertical walls of the reef as a backdrop. Lower Muddy Creek and an old mining track high above the canyon floor take you to Chimney Canyon with its luxuriant riparian side canyons and wondrously sculpted Wingate walls. The Pasture Track, an abandoned mining road, leads back to the trailhead. This route is a compilation of shorter routes that were first presented in *Canyoneering: The San Rafael Swell.*

Trip length:	Six days minimum. Layover days and digressions can add a day or two.
Elevation range:	4560′ to 5760′.
Recommended seasons:	March 15 to May 15 or before spring run-off, and September 1 to November 15. Water levels vary from year to year. Muddy Creek often dries up in July and August. Because there is so much wading on this trip, air temperatures should be reasonably warm before undertaking the hike. There is a flash flood potential in most of the canyons.
Maps:	7.5-series USGS topographic maps: Hunt Draw, The Frying Pan, and Tomsich Butte. Metric map: San Rafael Desert.

Skill level: This is a moderately strenuous route. The first day, hiking through The Chute, is the hardest and longest day. There is moderate route finding and there is one optional section of Class-4 climbing. Water may be scarce along some sections of the route. There may be one dry camp. There is a lot of wading on this route, but the water is rarely more than knee deep; however, there is the possibility of several short swims if water levels are high.

Special equipment: Wading shoes are essential. An old pair of hiking boots is recommended. Tennis shoes do not supply enough support. At least one inner tube per group should be carried for floating packs if water levels are high. Large plastic bags are indispensable for keeping equipment dry. Each member of the party should have a walking stick to probe for deep water. Sticks are available all along the river. The lead person should not carry a camera! A forty-foot rope will prove useful. Each hiker should have a minimum water-carrying capacity of six quarts. Even when the air is hot, the narrows can be chilly. Be prepared.

Notes: The Chute of Muddy Creek and Chimney Canyon are both highly favored destinations for backpackers. Carry out your toilet paper when in these areas.

It is recommended that you leave a water cache near the Hidden Splendor road. This is easy to do and will save you from having to carry water from Muddy Creek. Two gallons of water cached per person is suggested. Two food caches can also be placed along the route. Directions on where to place the caches are detailed in the road section. Rodents are not a big problem when placing food caches in the San Rafael Swell, but it is advisable to bury your food in plastic bags or containers. Remember to carry out your containers or retrieve them later. Erase all signs of your caches.

Administering agency: San Rafael Resource Area. Bureau of Land Management. 900 N. 700 E. Price, Utah 84501. (801-637-4584)

Land status: The Chute, upper Chimney Canyon, and Mud Canyon are in the Muddy Creek WSA. Cistern Canyon is in the

Crack Canyon WSA. Lower Muddy Creek from Hidden Splendor to its mouth and the lower mile of Chimney Canyon are state land. At the present time they are not protected. The Utah Wilderness Coalition proposal for wilderness designation areas includes all of the lands covered in this chapter.

ROAD SECTION

Access to Muddy Creek is via the Heart of Sinbad road. The road starts at the signed Goblin Valley exit on Highway 24, which is about twenty-five miles south of Interstate 70 and twenty-five miles north of Hanksville. This graded road is suitable for light-duty vehicles, but it may be impassable when wet. There is camping along spur roads. Driving time from either Hanksville or Interstate 70 to the trailhead is two hours. The road signs in the San Rafael Swell have a habit of disappearing from time to time, so keep track of mileage.

0.0 | —Mileage starts at Highway 24 and goes west. The road is paved.

5.1 | —Signed Goblin Valley junction. Continue straight (W) on the paved road.

6.0 | —Barrier Canyon–style pictograph panel under an overhang on the right (N). It can be seen from the road. These figures were drawn by Desert Archaic Indians sometime between 1000 B.C. and A.D. 500. You are now cutting through the Eastern Reef.

6.4 | —Road changes from asphalt to dirt.

7.1 | —A large parking area to the right (N) can be used for camping and as a base for exploring the Temple Mountain mining area.

7.2 | —"Tee." Stay on the main road to the right (W).

15.8	—Signed junction. Stay to the left (WNW). The road to the right goes to Interstate 70.
18.5	—Signed junction. Stay to the left (W). There is a sign to Reds Canyon and McKay Flat.
18.6	—Cattle guard.
19.3	—Signed junction. Go to the left (SW) toward McKay Flat.
27.5	—Signed junction. Stay to the right (NW). The road to the left (S) goes to the Hidden Splendor mining area. See the Hidden Splendor road section below for directions on where to place water and food caches.
31.0	—Cattle guard.
32.4	—"Tee." Go left (W) toward Hondoo Arch. The main road goes to the right (NE).
32.6	—Top of a small hill. Hondoo Arch is straight ahead. According to San Rafael historian Owen McClenahan, the name Hondoo is derived from the fancied and fanciful similarity between the arch and a knot on a cowboy's lariat, which is called a hondoo in Spanish. The monolith to the right is Tomsich Butte. Tomsich (also spelled Tomsick) was a uranium prospector. A story is told about Tomsich and his dog drinking poisonous creek water. Tomsich survived; the dog died.
32.8	—Two broken-down cabins to the left.
32.9	—The road divides. You can camp and park anywhere in this area. The hike starts at the end of the track to the left (S). There is no trail register. (The track is shown one-half mile southwest of Tomsich Butte on the **Tomsich Butte map**.)

> **Geology lesson:** The brown cliffs and towers that look like chocolate torte cakes are in the Moenkopi Formation. Look west across the river. The grayish slopes with mining tracks

running across them are in the Chinle Formation. Above the Chinle are vertical walls of Wingate Sandstone. The sloping ledges of the Kayenta Formation above the Wingate are nearly nonexistent in this area. The rounded domes at the top of the cliff are Navajo Sandstone.

Hidden Splendor road section. Directions for caching food and water.

0.0 —At the junction of the McKay Flats road and the Hidden Splendor road. This is at mile 27.5 above. There is a sign here. Go south.

5.2 —Old gray car on the left. The area to the left (E) is Sinbad Country. According to *Utah Place Names* author John W. Van Cott, Sinbad Country was named for its "arabesque monoliths of multiple shapes and colors representing scenes or castles described in the Arabian Knights." Wild horses and antelope are often seen in the area.

6.3 —Top of a hill. Good views into the Muddy Creek drainage. The area to the right (W) is called Keesle Country.

7.7 —There is a vague track to the left (ESE). It is north of a Wingate buttress and runs east behind the reef. (The track is not shown on the **Hunt Draw map**. It is located one-half mile north of elevation 6245T.) **(See Map Two.)** It may take some searching to find the track; which is impassable to most vehicles. You can cache food and water anywhere in the area. If you plan to explore Quandary, Ramp, or Upper Knotted Rope canyons, you will want to cache extra water here. (See *Canyoneering: The San Rafael Swell* for details.) You will reach this point on the middle of Day Two if no side trips are planned.

9.8 —The Hidden Splendor mining area. From the silver water tank follow a road west across an old airstrip to the edge of Muddy Creek. The road continues down to Muddy Creek, but you shouldn't try to drive it. Place your cache in the cliffs. You will reach this area at the end of Day Three if no side trips are planned.

Through The Chute of Muddy Creek.

Day One. 6.5 to 9.5 hours. If water levels are high, add another couple of hours. Tomsich Butte and Hunt Draw maps. There is water all day.

Down Muddy Creek

(**Tomsich Butte map** and **Map One.**) Go south down the canyon. Follow a mining track as you crisscross the creek. It is easiest to put on your wading shoes right at the start. The deeper into The Chute you progress, the more time you will spend in the water. Wilderness Study Area boundary markers appear in a half hour. Off-road vehicles are not allowed beyond this point. Minutes below the WSA boundary you will note the Pasture Track coming down a hillside to the right (LDC). The canyon starts to narrow and deepen. One hour from the WSA boundary signs, enter the first section of The Chute. (1.5–2.0 hours.)

> **Alternate route:** The first section of The Chute may contain several deep pools that require deep wading or short swims. If it seems unreasonable to proceed down The Chute, exit the canyon to the right (LDC)(W), negotiate a steep hillside (many options), and intersect the Pasture Track. Follow it south into Chimney Canyon, which is the first major drainage encountered. (**Hunt Draw map.**) Hike down Chimney Canyon for an hour to Muddy Creek to re-

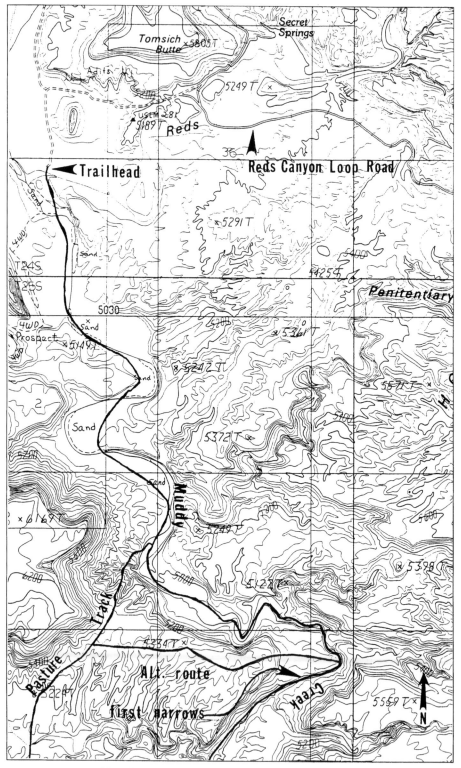

Map One

join the original route. There is a twin-tiered fall to descend near Muddy Creek (Class 4, 20′ and Class 4, 8′, belay and lower packs). (4.0–6.0 hours.)

Through The Chute

The canyon opens for a short distance after the first narrow section.

> **Digression:** After the first narrow section there is a Moenkopi-walled side canyon to the right (W) that is worth exploring. (0.5-hour round-trip.)

The canyon closes in again and the walls rise.

> **Rock-climber's note:** After a couple of hours, keep a look-out for a narrow side canyon to the left (LDC). It takes a bit of scrambling and some short stretches of climbing (Class 5.5, 20′) to get into. This is certainly one of the finest slots in the area. (0.5–1.0 hour round-trip.)

It takes four to six hours of constant wading to reach a log jam that is twenty-five feet above your head. (**Hunt Draw map.**) This is the narrowest portion of The Chute. It takes another hour to exit the narrows and reach the mouth of Chimney Canyon, which comes in on the right (NW). There is a ten-foot-high boulder on each side of Muddy Creek at its confluence with Chimney Canyon. Hike up Chimney Canyon for 200 yards and climb a short twin-tiered fall (Class 4, 8′ and Class 4, 20′, belay and haul packs). There is a large spring and good camping a couple of hundred yards above the falls. (5.0–7.5 hours.)

> **Historical note:** The name Chimney Canyon has been attributed to both the brick-colored walls of the Moenkopi Formation in the canyon's lower reaches and to a prominent, chimney-like tower near its head.

> **Water:** The preferred and prettier campsite is above the twin-tiered fall, but the springs there have a high mineral content and can cause stomach upset. An alternative is to camp at the mouth of Chimney Canyon and procure water from Muddy Creek. Cattle graze upstream, so treat the water with extra care. The use of this alternative negates the need to ascend the Class-4 wall at the twin-tiered fall.

Day Two. 5.5 to 8.0 hours. Hunt Draw map. There is no reliable water unless you have installed a water cache at the Hidden Splendor road.

To Mud Canyon

(**Hunt Draw map.**) Continue down Muddy Creek for forty-five minutes to the mouth of Mud Canyon. (**Map Two.**) It is the first side canyon coming in on the left (SE) at creek level. (Mud Canyon is shown but is not labeled on the map. It is located just north of elevation 5030T.) There will be no more water until the end of the day. If you did not place a water cache along the Hidden Splendor road, you will have to carry enough water to last until the middle of Day Three. Load up here. (1.0 hour.)

Up Mud Canyon

Hike up Mud Canyon. After thirty minutes the canyon divides at a ten-foot-high, brown, square tower that is at wash level on the right. Go left (N). Thirty minutes past the ten-foot tower the canyon divides at a brown mud fin. Go left (W). Follow the gray canyon floor.

> **Digression:** Go right, along the red canyon floor. This narrow canyon ends in an alcove. (0.25-hour round-trip.)

Fifteen minutes past the brown mud fin the canyon divides equally at a horizontally layered buttress. Go right (ENE). This section of canyon contains several challenging chockstones (Class 4) and ends at a fall. To exit the canyon, backtrack for 200 yards and scramble up a steep, loose slope to the left (LDC)(S). Below a dark-brown cliff band traverse left (E) at a comfortable level for five minutes. (Do not drop back into Mud Canyon.) Go around a corner and exit up the first easy break in the cliff band to the right. Hike to the top of the hill. (2.0–3.5 hours.)

Across Keesle Country

From the top of the hill look south-southeast toward a Wingate-topped buttress (elevation 6245T). You will see a mining track cutting across the Chinle on the northwest side of the buttress. Make your way toward the left side of the mining track. You will drop in and out of sev-

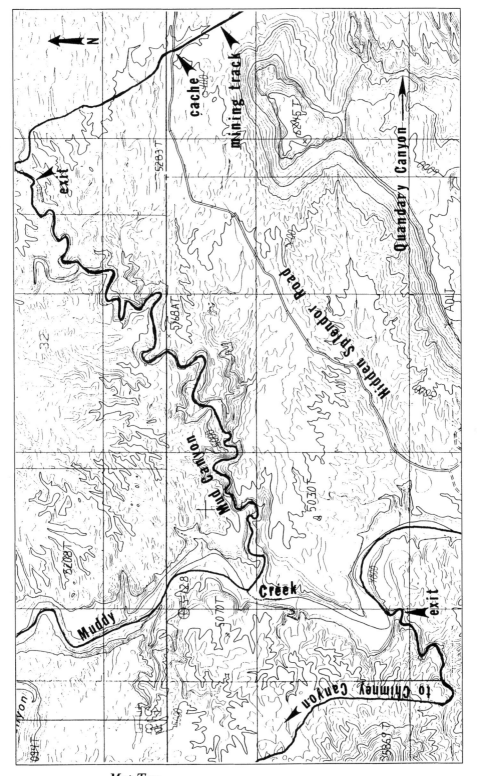

Map Two

Harvey Halpern and Bud Evans in Mud Canyon.

eral shallow canyons. All are easy to negotiate and variations here won't matter. Intersect the Hidden Splendor road (near elevation 5283T). (1.0 hour.)

To Cistern Canyon

Follow the Hidden Splendor road (the direction you take will depend on where you meet the road) until you intersect a vague mining track going east-southeast below the north side of the Wingate-walled buttress (elevation 6245T). Most hikers will have left a food and water cache in the vicinity.

Follow the mining track. In ten minutes the track passes an old car.

> **Digression:** There are three excellent canyoneering routes that start near here: Quandary, Upper Knotted Rope, and Ramp canyons. See *Canyoneering: The San Rafael Swell* for details.

Continue following the track southeast toward an opening in the escarpment to the right (S). The opening marks the head of Ramp Canyon. (Ramp Canyon is not labeled on the map. It is the first canyon going through the reef to the west of Cistern Canyon. It is immediately east of elevation 5650T.) There is good camping and medium potholes a short distance down Ramp Canyon.

Cistern Canyon is the first canyon to the east of Ramp Canyon. To get to it follow the track toward Ramp Canyon until you are close to its head, then go northeast up a steep slope. Stay parallel to a Wingate wall and below the Chinle. From the top of the slope follow a steep, shallow, red-walled gully east down to Cistern Canyon.

Hike south down Cistern Canyon to Bullberry Spring. There is good camping in an area of cottonwoods near this small spring. (1.5–2.5 hours.)

> **Water:** This is normally a dry camp. Water has to be carried from your cache near the Hidden Splendor road or from Muddy Creek. If you do not have enough water and Bullberry Spring is dry, continue south down Cistern Canyon. There are medium potholes throughout the canyon. If everything is dry, proceed to the large spring at the mouth of Quandary Canyon. See Day Three for details.

Day Three. 5.0 to 8.0 hours. Hunt Draw map. There is reliable water at the mouth of Quandary Canyon and in Muddy Creek.

Down Cistern Canyon

(**Hunt Draw map.**) Go south down Cistern Canyon. As the red Wingate walls rise, note the superb weathering of the sandstone. By the time you pass under a huge chockstone you are in the Navajo. The canyon itself presents small challenges but no big problems. You will pass through the Carmel Formation as you exit the Southern Reef. (1.0–1.5 hours.)

> **Geology lesson:** This is a good opportunity to take a minute to look at the Southern Reef. Note how the sandstone layers are tilted at an angle, at times almost reaching the vertical. These sandstone layers, or strata, were at one time horizontal. They were formed when the forces of wind and water carried sand from eastern highlands to their present location. The sand was deposited in freshwater lakes, along the shores of ancient seas, or in vast desert areas similar to the present-day Sahara. The unique characteristics of the various formations are due to the point of origin of the sand and silt and the diversity of the depositional environment.
>
> Fifty to sixty million years ago pressures like an expanding

Along the face of the Southern Reef.

balloon, from deep beneath the earth's crust pushed the strata upward, forming a dome-shaped anticline eighty miles long and forty miles wide. The area in the middle of the anticline is called the San Rafael Swell. The strata on the periphery of the anticline were pushed up to form the near-vertical walls that you are now looking at. The term "reef" is used to describe the escarpment because the early explorers who named it thought the walls looked like a coral reef.

To Muddy Creek

Your goal is to follow a wash southwest under the face of the reef to Muddy Creek. (Do not make the mistake of hiking south out the mouth of Cistern Canyon and continuing south into Hunt Draw.) There is a maze of small washes, hills, and cliffs. Try to stay in the main wash, but detour as necessary. (The wash is shown as a stream on the map.) It takes an hour to reach the mouth of Quandary Canyon, which comes in on the right (NW) (shown one-eighth mile northwest of elevation 4802T). It is easy to recognize since it is the only canyon in the area with large cottonwoods.

Digression: There are large pools a short way up Quandary Canyon. One is at the top of a steep slab. Although the mouth of the canyon is choked with vegetation, the pools are worth the trouble to reach them.

Continue southwest along the base of the reef for a half-hour to Muddy Creek. (1.5–2.5 hours.)

To Hidden Splendor

Follow Muddy Creek upcanyon. It cuts through the reef in an awesome display of Wingate and Navajo walls. There is a lot of wading, but even in high water the creek is usually no more than knee deep.

> **Digression:** The first side canyon to the right (E) after entering the reef is partially blocked by a wall of tamarisks. Five minutes up the side canyon is a large pool. Since you will be camping on Muddy Creek, you may want to obtain fresh water here. (The side canyon is shown one-quarter mile south of elevation 4990T.)

Mine shafts and an old building appear on the right (LUC) as you approach the Hidden Splendor mining area. (Hidden Splendor is not labeled on the map. It is one-half mile west of elevation 4888T.) A couple of tracks run east up the cliffs to the mine site, but there isn't much to see. (2.0–3.0 hours.)

> **Historical note:** Vernon Pick, a novice prospector from Minnesota, discovered uranium at Hidden Splendor in 1952. The story of his discovery is interesting. After a business setback in Minnesota, Pick and his wife decided to move to California. On the way, he heard about the uranium rush in Utah. Hoping to get in on the boom, Pick drove to Hanksville. He spent six months searching without success for uranium near the San Rafael Swell.
>
> Nearly out of money, Vernon decided to give prospecting one last try before continuing on to the coast. He examined Crack and Chute canyons, then headed for Muddy Creek. He was only able to drive to within fifteen miles of the creek, so he hiked cross-country the rest of the way. Muddy Creek was swollen by recent rains and, after a struggle, Pick finally reached the Hidden Splendor area.
>
> Using his scintillometer—a type of Geiger counter— Pick discovered a fertile lode of uranium-bearing ore. After marking his claim, which he named the Delta Mine, he

headed back to Hanksville to record it. Muddy Creek was still running high. Pick built a crude raft and floated part of the way down the creek before his raft disintegrated after hitting a rock. Now on foot and sick from drinking arsenic-laced water, he barely made it back to his truck.

Vernon Pick built the road from McKay Flats down to the Delta Mine. After extracting a million dollars worth of ore, he sold the mine to Floyd Odlum for ten million dollars in 1954. Odlum changed the mine's name to Hidden Splendor; he then found that the mine was played out. Until the debacle was forgotten, the mine was called Odlum's Hidden Blunder.

Years later, Vernon Pick was asked about his lucky discovery. He said: "The trouble with most people is that they don't like to walk. They want to go where they can drive a car or ride a horse. To get into the places where I wanted to go—the places nobody else had been—there was no choice but walking. And I walked plenty."

To the exit canyon

Continue up Muddy Creek. Follow a mining track where possible and ford the creek as necessary. Twenty-five minutes from Hidden Splendor, where the canyon makes a U-turn and goes from south to north, the first side canyon enters on the left (S) (shown one-quarter mile north of elevation 5975T). **(Map Two.)** The floor of the side canyon is covered with rounded stream rocks. This side canyon and the main canyon to the north are both in the Muddy Creek WSA and are closed to off-road vehicles. There is camping on sandy benches on both sides of the creek. (0.5–1.0 hour.)

> **Water:** Cattle graze throughout the area, so treat the water with extra care.

Day Four. 3.5 to 5.0 hours. Hunt Draw and The Frying Pan maps. There is no reliable water along the route. There is a large spring at the end of the day.

To Chimney Canyon

(Hunt Draw map.) Go up the side canyon to the south. There will be no more wading for a couple of days. An old mining track appears in the streambed. Follow it out the right (LUC) side of the canyon, then north past the Little Susan Mine site. There are fine views of Keesle Country on the far side of the Muddy Creek Gorge to the east. Continue north on the track to Chimney Canyon. There are medium springs a short stroll downcanyon. (2.0–3.0 hours.)

Up Chimney Canyon

Hike up Chimney Canyon along a wide wash surrounded by towering Wingate and Navajo walls. If you are cutting corners (which you can do), you will cross an abandoned airstrip that is not on the map. (**The Frying Pan map.**) Past the airstrip, at the junction of the South and North forks of Chimney Canyon, there is an old miner's cabin and a chicken coop (one-quarter mile southwest of elevation 5834). There is camping near the cabin as well as farther up the South Fork. See Day Five for details. (1.5–2.0 hours.)

> **Water:** There is a large spring 100 yards behind the cabin in the South Fork.

Day Five. This is a day to explore the North and South forks of Chimney Canyon. Photographers may want to spend a couple of days in these canyons. The Frying Pan map. There are large springs scattered throughout all of these canyons.

Exploring the South Fork

(**The Frying Pan map.**) To get into the South Fork, which is the canyon behind the cabin, hike southwest up the narrow mouth of the canyon for a hundred yards and tackle a short pour-off (Class 4+, 10′). If this is too difficult or wet, follow the main canyon north for several hundred yards to an old mining track that goes through a break in the wall to the left (LUC). Ascend the mining track and hike into the South Fork.

Above the pour-off the canyon divides. Go right (W). There are many shady campsites in an area of large spring-fed pools. As you dayhike farther up the canyon, there are small obstacles and incredible rewards. Colors and textures run rampant here, and the Wingate walls have been

The Little Susan Mine. Photo by Harvey Halpern.

elegantly etched by wind and water. Above a fall, the canyon floor stretches white and sandy. Look for Halloween Hollow (AN), a small side canyon or slot to the right (LUC). Its walls of dripping sandstone have been compared to Antoni Gaudí's gothic cathedral—Sagrada Familia—in Barcelona, Spain. The main canyon ends at a pool and hanging garden. (1.0–2.0 hours round-trip.)

The left fork of the South Fork has large springs and

contains a large triple arch on the left (E) that is about twenty minutes upcanyon. You will have to look downcanyon in order to spot it. (1.0 hour round-trip.)

Exploring the North Fork

Go north from the cabin. In ten minutes there is a short, wide canyon to the right that is not very interesting. In twenty minutes the main canyon divides at a red buttress that is covered with small holes. Go left (SSW). After ten minutes note the Ghoul's Wall (AN) to the right (LUC). (If you go too far, you will run into a balanced dirt clod in the middle of the streambed. Backtrack for a hundred yards.) There are wonderfully monstrous and imaginative shapes formed in the eroding sandstone. This is the best wall of its type that I have seen. After another ten minutes the canyon ends at a fall.

> **Rock-climber's note:** The canyon ends only for non-climbers. For climbers there is a special treat ahead. Because the next section of canyon is difficult to enter from either end, it is pristine. Backtrack from the fall for several hundred yards until the wall to the right (LDC)(S) reaches its lowest height. Find the easiest place to ascend the wall (Class 5.3, 20′, belay). Above the fall the canyon divides. Go right. The canyon ends in a fine set of narrows and a small grotto.

Return to the canyon division that is ten minutes down the canyon from the Ghoul's Wall. Go left (LDC)(N). This short canyon complex is the music of Chimney Canyon. Plan on at least an hour to explore these lavishly vegetated masterpieces. Because of the intense beauty of these side canyons, do not camp in them. Please leave them absolutely unscarred. (2.0–3.0 hours round-trip.)

Day Six. 5.0 to 7.0 hours. The Frying Pan, Hunt Draw, and Tomsich Butte maps. There is no reliable water until the end of the day.

To the Pasture Track

(The Frying Pan map.) From the miner's cabin backtrack down Chimney Canyon. Several hundred yards

Sculpted walls, Chimney Canyon.

south of the southern or downcanyon end of the abandoned airstrip you need to locate an indistinct mining track coming in from the left (E). This is the Pasture Track. It is hard to see and may take some looking to find.

Along the Pasture Track

The track initially goes east and parallels the streambed. **(Hunt Draw map.)** It then turns north and traverses The Pasture. (The track turns north near elevation 5133T.) The Pasture Track stays high above Muddy Creek and runs along the top or west side of the pasture area well below the Wingate and Chinle.

Two hours from Chimney Canyon there is a wide side canyon coming in on the left (W) (shown to the south of elevation 5224T on the **Tomsich Butte map**). There are old mine workings at the head of the canyon that are not visible from the track. A small spring is located fifty yards downcanyon from the Pasture Track.

Fifteen minutes past the side canyon the track "Tees." The track you want to follow branches off to the right and enters a gully going southeast. This "Tee" is nearly impossible to see. Look for a cairn on a peninsula to the right (LUC). (If you don't see the "Tee," the track you are on will take you to the edge of a very steep slope. The correct track will be 100 feet below. Slide down the slope—not

The Pasture Track.

fun with a pack on—or backtrack and find the Pasture Track.) Follow the track down to Muddy Creek, then walk and wade upcanyon to the trailhead at Tomsich Butte. (5.0–7.0 hours.)

Ginger

Ginger Harmon and I met while on a trip through Parunaweep Canyon near Zion National Park. The first thing I noticed about Ginger was her bulging "Captain America"–shaped calves. "This woman has done some hiking!" I thought to myself. Over the years I have learned how right I was. It is a rare mountain range or canyon floor that Ginger has not explored. From the Sierra Nevada to the peaks of the Himalayas, from the canyons of Utah to the gorges of the Sinai, Ginger has been there. While many Grand Canyon hikers count their time under the rim in days, Ginger calculates hers in years. Most hikers or climbers are happy walking the trails or ascending established routes, but Ginger finds the most satisfaction in exploring the unknown. She can be credited with new routes both in the canyons and in the mountains.

Although Ginger is retired, she is no fainéant: she is active in helping preserve the few wildlands we have left. Ginger is a founding member of Great Old Broads For Wilderness, a lobbying group composed of women over the age of forty-five. She is also a board member of the Southern Utah Wilderness Alliance.

I was pleased when Ginger agreed to spend a couple of weeks one winter hiking with me in the Dirty Devil. I had spent several months searching out routes in the upper portions of the Devil but had not had a chance to put together a loop trip. Our goal was to hike north from Twin Corral Box to Robbers Roost Canyon without wading along the river. The route-finding challenge across the slickrock and over the plateau areas between canyons was intricate and enticing. The two times we had to cross the river were both trials. The river was swollen by melted snow and we had to dodge ice flows as we waded through the waist-deep water.

The trip was a success. However, Ginger had not seen enough of Dirty Devil country. While we had concentrated on finding reasonably sane routes through the canyons, we had also been eyeing the plethora of narrow slots that form a ring around the upper reaches of Robbers Roost Canyon.

At a meeting in Salt Lake City a year later, Ginger suggested that we take a closer look at those slots. She had flown up from her home in Tucson and was ill-equipped for a winter outing, but after borrowing and buying the necessary gear, we headed south.

Over a two-week period we managed to descend a half-dozen slot canyons. All required rope work and teamwork. Some required swimming across potholes in below-freezing weather. One canyon in particular stands out in memory. We named it the Mind Bender Fork of the North Fork of Robbers Roost Canyon. The upper part of the canyon went smoothly; Ginger and I swapped leads as we worked downcanyon. Claustrophobic narrows were interspersed with vertical challenges: the occasional rappel, a thirty-foot-tall bombay chimney (the farther down we climbed the wider the chimney got), and a sheer wall with few holds.

By the time we reached the crux section of the canyon, we had been enveloped by a blizzard; the snow that whipped through the canyon stung our eyes and froze our hands. The crux was truly a mind bender; the narrow slot gave way to an abrupt drop over the 155-foot-high mouth of a huge cave. We spent an hour rigging our ropes. With no secure anchor points, we ended up burying a sling under a pile of rocks at the bottom of a large pothole and attaching the rope to it.

I went first, carefully sliding out of the slot and into a vertical void, the floor of the canyon invisible in the swirl of snow. Would the rope be long enough? The question was answered when I was halfway down: the rope was long enough but my trajectory would have taken me through the limbs of an oak tree and into a large pool. Not good! With some gentle swinging I managed to hit a dry landing zone. Ginger took her time lowering packs over the fifteen-story drop. From below I saw that the brunt of the storm had descended on her. The rock was

Ginger after the descent of the Mind Bender Fork of Robbers Roost Canyon.

now plastered with rime ice and, perilously perched on the edge of the abyss, every move on her part had to be carefully executed. A mistake could have meant the ultimate splat. At long last I saw Ginger's legs emerge from the slot; she slowly spun down the rope, afraid a sudden jerk would dislodge it from its precarious anchor. There were no further impediments below. The Mind Bender Fork was a done deal.

The Dirty Devil North

It is a lonely and terrible wilderness, such a wilderness as Christ and the prophets went out into; harshly and beautifully colored, broken and worn until its bones are exposed, its great sky without a smudge or taint from Technocracy, and in hidden corners and pockets under its cliffs the sudden poetry of springs.

Wallace Stegner, on Robbers Roost country—1960

General description: The Dirty Devil River Gorge has only recently come to the attention of backpackers. This is perhaps due to its quiet demeanor and its proximity to the ever-popular Maze District of Canyonlands National Park. Starting near Hanksville at the confluence of the Fremont River and Muddy Creek, the Dirty Devil cuts through a great variety of ever-changing sandstone formations in its serpentine forty-mile-long course to Lake Powell.

While the main canyon is stunning, it is the side canyons that are the real attraction. Each is distinctive, not only in ambience but in geologic aspect as well. Starting in the north, sand-floored Robbers Roost Canyon and its many slot-like tributaries cut through Navajo Sandstone. Continuing south, the walls of No Mans Canyon are dominated by the Kayenta Formation, dark red and sullen overhead. Larry Canyon contains an artist's fantasy of whimsically carved designs on its Wingate walls. As one moves south again, Twin Corral Box and Sams Mesa Box canyons are also dominated by Wingate Sandstone, with the Chinle Formation forming the canyon floors. (The next series of canyons to the south—Happy, Hatch, and Fiddler Cove—is covered in the Dirty Devil South chapter.)

The northern part of the Dirty Devil River area was in-

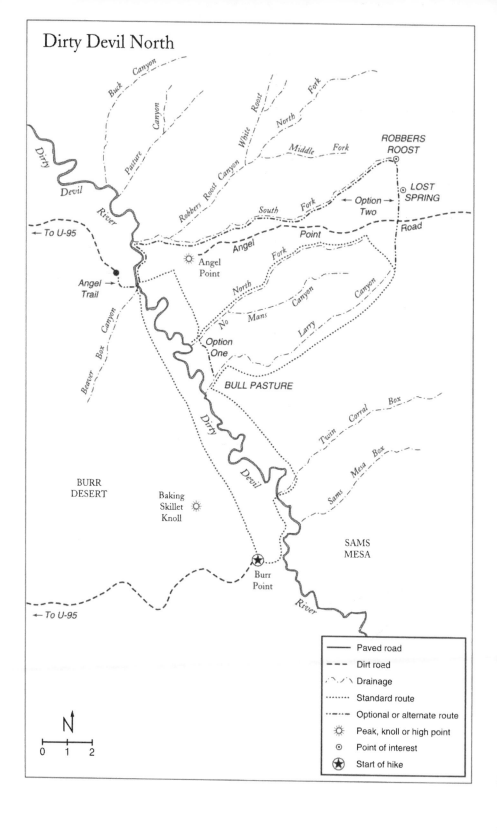

habited by Desert Archaic Indians from 5500 B.C. to A.D. 500. They left Barrier Canyon–style pictograph panels in an alcove across the river from the mouth of Robbers Roost Canyon. Fremont Indians lived in the canyons of the Dirty Devil from A.D. 500 to 1300. Signs of their presence can be found in the caves along the lower reaches of No Mans Canyon, at rock art panels in most of the tributary canyons, and in the rows of Moqui steps they chiseled in the walls of Pasture and Larry canyons.

Mormon ranchers arrived in the area in the late 1800s. Toward the end of that century they shared their lands with the outlaws of Robbers Roost. In the 1950s and 1960s, uranium prospectors shredded the landscape in a futile search for wealth. They left a network of abandoned roads and several glory holes.

The route is designed to minimize wading; there are only two river crossings in seven days. The hike starts at Burr Point, drops 1,500 feet to the Dirty Devil, and crosses the river at Twin Corral Box. After exiting Twin Corral Box, the route stays high above the river, then drops into Larry Canyon. From there the route goes overland to the head of the North Fork of No Mans Canyon. An interesting journey down No Mans Canyon and to the Angel Trail leads back to the river near Robbers Roost Canyon. The loop is completed with a hike along the west rim of the Dirty Devil Gorge back to Burr Point.

Trip length: Seven days minimum. Layover days, digressions, and options can add several more days to the length of the trip.

Elevation range: 3980′ to 5600′.

Recommended seasons: March 1 to June 1 and September 15 to December 1.

Maps: 7.5-series USGS topographic maps: Angel Cove, Angel Point, Baking Skillet Knoll, and Burr Point. A Robbers Roost Flats map is needed if you plan to do Option Two.

The Point of Rocks East map is needed if you plan to do Option Three.
Metric map: Hanksville.

Skill level: This is a moderately strenuous route. There is difficult route finding and Class-4+ climbing. The leader must be familiar with belay techniques and be capable of leading the climbing sections without protection. There are several places with lots of exposure. Water may be scarce on some stretches depending on the season. There are two dry camps. The optional descent of the South Fork of Robbers Roost Canyon is technical. See Option Two for details.

Special equipment: Wading shoes are optional, as there are only two river crossings. A fifty-foot climbing rope is adequate.

Notes: Although much of this country has few visitors, Robbers Roost Canyon is becoming increasingly popular. Those visiting Robbers Roost Canyon should carry out their toilet paper. Camp fires are allowed, but please do not use them.

Administering agency: Henry Mountains Resource Area. Bureau of Land Management. 406 S. 100 W. Hanksville, Utah 84734. (801-542-3461.)

Land status: Most of the lands covered in this hike are in the Dirty Devil WSA. Some of the plateau areas above the canyons have been left out of the BLM proposal. The Utah Wilderness Coalition proposal for wilderness designation areas includes all of the lands covered in this chapter.

ROAD SECTION

The signed road to the Burr Point trailhead starts 15.6 miles south of Hanksville on Highway 95. (Hanksville is at 0 mile. There are signs every mile.) The graded road is suitable for light-duty vehicles but may be impassable when wet. There is camping on spur roads. Driving time from Hanksville to the trailhead is one hour.

0.0	—Mileage starts at Highway 95 and goes east.
1.6	—Spigot on the left.
1.7	—"Y." Go right (NE).
2.1	—View into Poison Spring Canyon to the right (E).
2.6	—Cattle guard.
3.5	—"Tee." Corral to the right. Stay left.
4.3	—"Y." Go right (SE).
5.7	—"Tee." Go left (NE).
7.6	—"Y." Go right (NE).
7.9	—Stock pond on the left.
10.0	—"Y." Go left (NE).
10.2	—The Burr Point trailhead is at a drill pipe at the edge of a cliff. There is plenty of room for parking and camping. There is no trail register. (The drill pipe is shown as DH to the east of elevation 5530T on the **Burr Point map**.)

> **Geology lesson:** All of the formations you will encounter on the hike are visible from the parking area. You are standing on a thin layer of the Carmel Formation. The slickrock immediately below you, and the prominent towers across the gorge to the east, are Navajo Sandstone. The dark red, ledge-forming cliffs below the Navajo are the Kayenta Formation. The tall, conspicuous vertical walls below the Kayenta are Wingate Sandstone. The grayish slopes below the Wingate, and the flat area near the river with a track running across it, are in the Chinle Formation. The thin, even-bedded, brown cliffs downcanyon at river level are in the Moenkopi Formation.

Historical note: Hanksville was named for Ebeneazer Hanks, who moved to the area in 1882. Before his arrival, the town was variously called Graves Valley, Pleasant Creek, or Floral. Hanksville is the closest settlement to Robbers Roost country and was used by the Wild Bunch for procuring supplies. In 1954 author Robert Coughlan described Hanksville: "One comes upon it with disbelief: a speck of stubborn protoplasm amidst the vastness of the desert, surrounded by drifting sands, stupendous buttes, grotesque red sandstone shapes and arid washes filled with loose, bone-dry pebbles."

Some may wish to shorten the hike by leaving a car at the top of the Angel Trail.

The unsigned road to the Angel Trail trailhead starts 5.3 miles south of Hanksville on Highway 95. This graded road is suitable for high-clearance vehicles, but may be impassable when wet. There are several long stretches of sand that can cause problems. There is camping along spur roads. Driving time from Hanksville to the trailhead is forty-five minutes.

0.0 —Mileage starts at Highway 95 and the route goes south-southeast. There is a stop sign. Short orange posts have been installed at some of the intersections. Always follow the road with the orange post.

0.4 —"Y." Vague track to the right. Stay on the main road to the left (SE).

0.9 —Barbed-wire corral on the right.

2.1 —The reddish slickrock to the left is Entrada Sandstone.

3.3 —"Y." Go left (N).

4.7 —"Y." Road to the left (E) goes to a wood corral. Stay with the main road to the right (NE). There is an orange post at the intersection.

8.0 —"Y." Stay with the main road to the right (ENE).

8.7 —"Tee." Track coming in on the left (E). Stay with the main road to the right (SE). There is a small, round water tank just past the junction.

8.8 —Down a steep hill.

9.2 —"Tee." Track coming in on the left (E). Stay with the main road to the right (SSE).

9.5 —"Tee." Turn left (SE) off the main road onto a track. There is an orange post at the intersection.

9.8 —Angel Trail trailhead. There is a limited amount of parking and camping on the crest of a ridge. There is no trail register. (The trailhead is located near the junction of a Pack Trail, a 4WD track, and a road to the east of Angel Cove on the **Angel Cove map.**)

Day One. 5.0 to 6.0 hours. Burr Point map. There is no reliable water until the end of the day.

To the Dirty Devil

(**Burr Point map** and **Map Three.**) Walk east from the drill pipe to the edge of the cliff. Skirt south along the rim for 100 yards to a trail that cuts diagonally across a sandy area and down a steep slab. At the bottom of the slab proceed north-northeast for a couple of minutes to the top of the first slickrock dome. One-third mile further to the north-northeast are two domes: the one to the left is yellowish; the one to the right is reddish and is covered with boulders. Cross slickrock until you come to the right (E) side of the reddish dome, then go northeast to the rim of the canyon. Find a red tower with a red top below the edge of the cliff to the left (NE). There are several red towers in the vicinity; the one you seek is the only one without vegetation on its summit. From the saddle between the red tower and the main cliff, downclimb a wall and a steep slab to the north (Class 4).

Traverse generally north on a Kayenta bench along a hiker-developed path. This is an old Fremont Indian route. After about one and a half hours the bench widens considerably. The closest canyon across the river to the

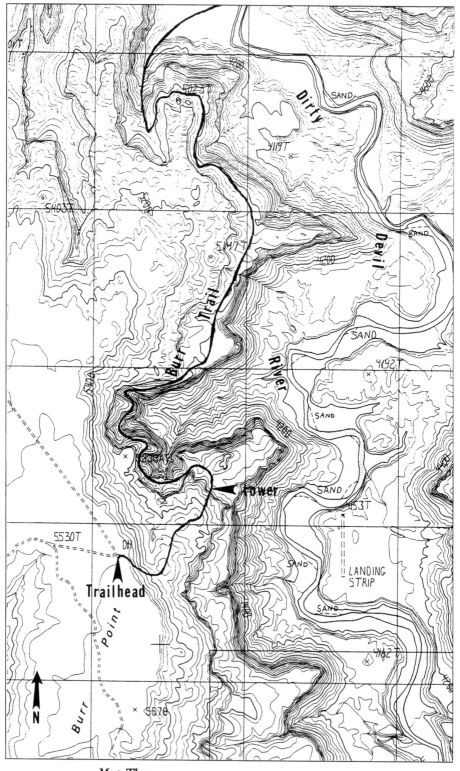

Map Three

east is Sams Mesa Box. As the bench narrows again, Twin Corral Box comes into view a mile upcanyon from Sams Mesa Box. The path goes to the head of a side canyon that empties into the Dirty Devil River opposite Twin Corral Box (shown to the west of elevation 5023T). Descend this steep, Wingate-walled canyon by starting on its east side, 100 yards down from the apex. Pass the first fall on the right, then the second on the left. The difficulty eases as you enter the Chinle. Cross the Dirty Devil opposite Twin Corral Box. The river is rarely more than knee deep. (4.5–5.5 hours.)

Historical note: The Dirty Devil River was named by members of the first John Wesley Powell expedition down the Green and Colorado rivers in 1869. Powell wrote: ". . . we discovered the mouth of a stream which enters from the right. Into this our little boat is turned. One of the men in the boat following, seeing what we have done, shouts to Dunn, asking if it is a trout stream. Dunn replies, much disgusted, that it is 'a dirty devil' and by this name the river is to be known hereafter."

The muddy water of the Dirty Devil prompted many explorers to comment on its quality. Jack Sumner, a member of the second Powell expedition in 1871, wrote: ". . . we rowed into camp just below a side stream coming in from the north which stinks bad enough to be the sewer from Sodom and Gomorrah, or even hell." Ellsworth Kolb, on a trip down the Colorado River from Wyoming to Mexico in 1911, described the Dirty Devil as "muddy and alkaline, while warm springs containing sulphur and other minerals added to its unpalatable taste."

The name Twin Corral Box comes from twin corrals that Cap Brown, a horse thief who roamed the area in the 1870s, built on the plateau above the canyon. The area is now called Twin Corral Flats.

Up Twin Corral Box

Ramble northeast up Twin Corral Box. After twenty minutes there is a stunning 150-foot pinnacle on a Wingate ridge to the left. **(Map Four.)** Nine minutes past the pinnacle locate a steep talus slope leading to a wide Wingate-walled chute or bowl to the left (WNW). From the canyon floor the chute does not look like it will go. The

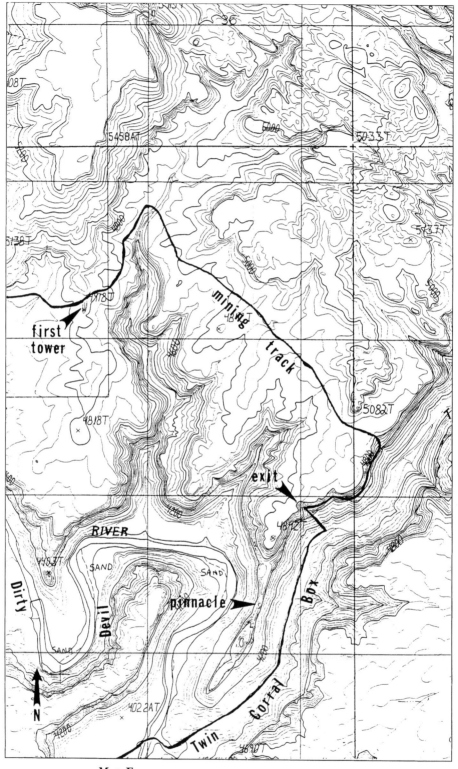

Map Four

chute is the exit route. (The chute is shown as an indent in the canyon wall one-eighth mile northeast of elevation 4842T.) There is good camping in the area. (0.5 hours.)

Water: Continue up the main canyon for thirty-five minutes until it divides. Hike up the left (N) fork for fifteen minutes to a large spring in a grove of cottonwoods. The camping is poor in this area.

Day Two. 5.5 to 8.5 hours. Burr Point and Angel Point maps. There is no reliable water along the route until the end of the day.

Exit Twin Corral Box

(Burr Point map.) Hike up the steep talus slope and through the Wingate chute to the Kayenta (Class 4+, belay and hand up packs as necessary). Traverse right (E) along a sloping Kayenta ledge for twenty minutes to the first easy exit out of the canyon. Proceed west toward a Navajo tower (elevation 5082T) and intersect an old mining track. (The track is not shown on the map.) (1.0–1.5 hours.)

Rock-climber's note: There is a more difficult, technical, and exciting exit out of Twin Corral Box. Thirty minutes past the 150-foot pinnacle a short, steep canyon comes in on the left (N) (shown one-quarter mile northeast of elevation 5082T). There is a jumble of boulders near the bottom of the canyon and a vertical rib between the Wingate walls toward the top.

Toil up the initial boulder-choked slope. At the Wingate, ascend a chimney filled with loose rock on the right (Class 5.0, 30′, belay. Packs can be hauled up a vertical cliff to the left.) Above, a difficult move around a large chockstone can be avoided by squeezing through a hole. The next cliff is ascended by using large holds on a steep prow (Class 5.1, 20′, belay). The major difficulties are over. There is a mining track on a Kayenta bench at the top of the canyon. Follow it south, then northwest around a Navajo point (elevation 5082T) and join the standard route. (Add 1.0–2.0 hours.)

Exiting Twin Corral Box.

To Larry Canyon

Go north on the mining track. It passes through three low saddles, each with a dome or tower to the left. (**Map Five.**) The third tower is the most impressive—a 100-foot shaft of Navajo Sandstone. (The first tower is elevation 4918T; the second is elevation 5162T; the third tower is one-quarter mile east-southeast of elevation 4805T). To

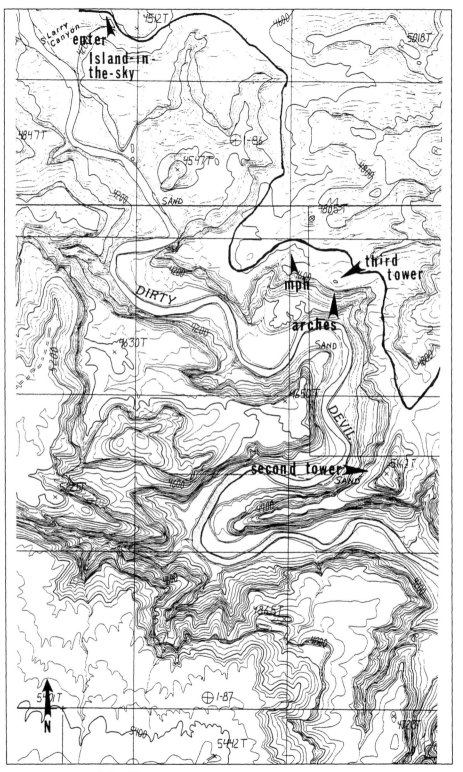

Map Five

the west of the third tower is a slickrock sheet with a shallow drainage running through it toward the river. There are medium potholes in the drainage near the edge of the cliff. Southwest of the tower are two large arches on the rim of the canyon. (2.0–3.0 hours.)

> **Digression:** With some searching, this drainage provides access to the river (Class 4).

The track becomes harder to follow. After a half hour it goes by a fine viewpoint above an abandoned meander (elevation 4547T). Five minutes later a wide canyon (Bull Pasture) comes in on the right (E). The mining track turns up Bull Pasture. Do not follow it; instead, continue traversing northwest. In five minutes there is an "island in the sky" to the west with a bridge running to it. (It is one-quarter mile south of elevation 4512T.) Without a pack, walk to the northwest corner of the "island." Look north into a side canyon and locate a route that traverses the Kayenta to a rock-slide going down the Wingate into Larry Canyon (Class 3). (1.5–2.5 hours.)

Up Larry Canyon

Walk up heavily sculpted Larry Canyon. **(Angel Point map.)** The best examples of this type of erosion seem to be confined to Wingate Sandstone. In twenty-five minutes a side canyon with a huge cave comes in on the right (E).

> **Alternate route:** A cattle trail exits the top of this side canyon and provides an alternate (and easier) route out of Larry Canyon to the exit described below.

After another thirty-five minutes the canyon becomes very busy. It narrows a tad and the Wingate walls become unbelievable. Steep gullies come in on either side of the canyon. There is an intermittent flow of water. Note the balanced boulder in the middle of the streamed on the left (LUC) side of the canyon. This marks the point where you will exit the canyon. Large cottonwoods make this an ideal spot to camp. (1.0–1.5 hours.)

> **Water:** If water is not flowing in this part of the canyon,

there are large springs in both forks of Larry Canyon. See Dayhiking in Larry Canyon on Day Three.

Day Three. 1.5 to 3.0 hours with backpacks. Angel Point map. Larry Canyon has large springs. The day ends at a dry camp.

Note: This is a short day with backpacks. There is plenty of time to dayhike in both forks of Larry Canyon.

Option: See Option One for a description of a direct route between Larry and No Mans canyons.

Dayhiking in Larry Canyon

(Angel Point map.) Three minutes up from the balanced boulder the canyon divides; the main channel goes to the right (SE).

Digression: The canyon to the left (NE) has a large spring. As you work up the canyon note the occasional lenses of a Moenkopi-type formation sandwiched between the Wingate and the Kayenta. The canyon ends at a fall after fifteen minutes.

Follow the main canyon for fifteen minutes to a beautiful area of cottonwoods and large springs. The canyon ends at a pool under a huge chockstone. Glorious. (2.0–4.0 hours round-trip.)

Exit Larry Canyon

Note: You can camp in Larry Canyon on the night of Day Three, but it is better to jump-start Day Four, which is long on miles and in vertical gain. There are also obstacles to overcome and a possible lack of water along the route. The next reliable water source is in the North Fork of No Mans Canyon, which you will reach at the end of Day Four. Load up with water here.

From the balanced boulder go downcanyon for a couple of hundred yards until you pass a gully that comes in from the left (LDC)(SE). (The gully is one-quarter mile north of elevation 4898T. The exit route starts due south of the "y" in Larry.) Zigzag south up the Kayenta wall to the right of the gully (Class 3+). Try to follow a deer trail. If you find lots of exposure under your boots, you have not found the easiest way. There may be a place or two where you will need to lift packs.

Near the top of the Kayenta, and below the Navajo, intersect a cattle trail and follow it to the left (E) (under elevation 4898T). Within ten minutes you pass over a small saddle. There is good camping along the rim of Larry Canyon, with exceptional views into its upper recesses. (1.5–3.0 hours.)

Water: This is a dry camp. Water has to be hauled from the springs in Larry Canyon.

Day Four. 6.5 to 8.5 hours. Angel Point map. There is no reliable water until the end of the day.

To the head of Larry Canyon

(Angel Point map.) From the saddle drop east to a small dune area and into a shallow wash. This is Bull Pasture. Follow the wash upcanyon (E). In twelve minutes there is a quarter-mile-long canyon to the left (NE). On its left (W) side are the faint remains of an old track going up a hill. You will have to look downcanyon in order to spot the track. (The track is shown as a Pack Trail on the map.)

Follow the Pack Trail north. If you have any doubts, they should be dispelled by a stone fence at the top of the first hill. After thirty-five minutes the Pack Trail cuts across the Navajo on a constructed ledge. A short, steep slickrock gully to the right (shown to the south of elevation 5060T) contains medium potholes. The track continues up the Navajo and tops out on the Carmel. (2.0–2.5 hours.)

The views from the top are terrific. To the:

North-northwest: The low flat-topped mesas are the Flat Tops.
Northwest: The San Rafael Swell and Reef with the Wasatch Plateau in the background.

West-northwest: Factory Butte with Thousand Lake Mountain in the background.
West: Capitol Reef with the north end of Boulder Mountain in the background.
Southwest: The Henry Mountains. The tallest peak on the north end is Mount Ellen (11,506′).
South-southwest: The Little Rockies are in the distance.

Historical note: Early explorers called the Henry Mountains the Unknown, Dirty Devil, or Our mountains. John Wesley Powell renamed them in honor of Joseph Henry, the secretary of the Smithsonian Institution who contributed to the success of the Powell expeditions down the Colorado River. Mount Ellen was named for Ellen Thompson, Powell's sister. Her husband, Almon, was second-in-command on the Powell expedition of 1871.

The Pack Trail has now turned into a seldom-used track. Follow it northeast for a half hour or so (time discrepancies don't matter here); then, for aesthetic reasons only, cut north to the rim of Larry Canyon. Staying on the Carmel, hike to the head of Larry Canyon (one-quarter mile north of elevation 5630). Note a line of Moqui steps on the left (LDC) wall of Larry Canyon fifty yards down from its apex. (1.5–2.0 hours.)

Option: For those seeking a livelier and more technical route, see Option Two for a description of a route variation that starts here and goes down the South Fork of Robbers Roost Canyon.

To the North Fork of No Mans Canyon

Head northwest. At the top of the first rise pick a landmark in the distance to use as a guidepost—the right-hand side of Factory Butte works well—and cross a blackbrush-littered plain. The goal is to find the top of the North Fork of No Mans Canyon. **(Map Six.)** This is the canyon that parallels, and is directly south of, the road going out to Angel Point. Pass the heads of several canyons. It does get confusing. It is perhaps easiest to plan to intersect the Angel Point road, then backtrack several hundred yards to the head of the North Fork. (1.0–1.5 hours.)

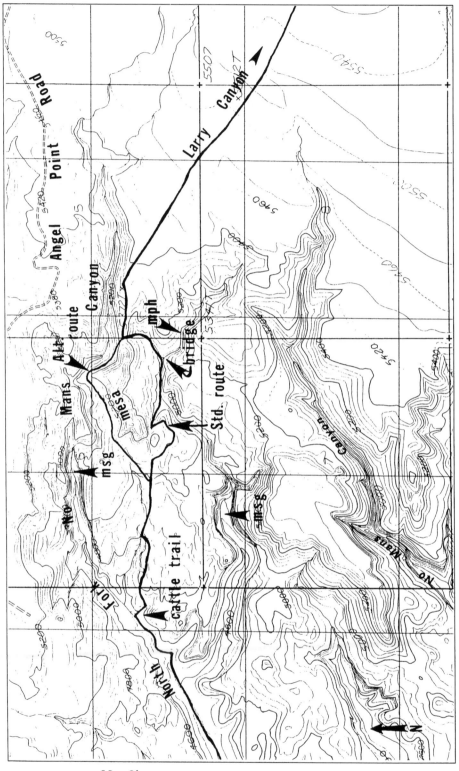

Map Six

Marcey Olajos and friends in slot canyon near the Angel Trail.

Into the North Fork

Once at the head of the North Fork of No Mans Canyon, go west along its south rim (passing over elevation 5372T). After twenty minutes your westward progress is thwarted by a short cliff. To the west is a ridge with two thirty-foot formations and behind them a small Navajo mesa. (On the map the mesa has a marked 5,200-foot contour line on its north side.) Find a way west down the cliff onto the ridge, past the towers and a small dome, and into a saddle immediately below the east side of the small mesa.

Descend a steep slab to the left (S) into a sandy bowl. Go west down the narrow canyon. (If there have been recent rains and the canyon has too much water in it, use the alternate route described below.) The first section is very narrow, then opens, and later narrows again. At the end of the second narrow section there is a small natural bridge.

> **Rock-climber's note:** The slot behind the bridge contains several interesting sections. The chimney moves required to get over a large chockstone will test the mettle of most (Class 5.5, 25'). There are medium potholes in the slot.

The canyon opens again. Look west. Note that the mesa ends in a notch with a rounded dome on its left (W)

Hansjörg Wyss on the cattle trail into the North Fork of No Mans Canyon.

side. Negotiate another section of narrows, then ascend a steep chute until you reach a conspicuous limestone ledge below the notch. (If you go too far downcanyon, you will encounter an impressive drop.) Follow the ledge south, then west, until the North Fork becomes visible. To the west you will see a short and wide side canyon or bay.

Proceed to the head of the side canyon, then skirt left (SW) along the rim of the main canyon for a couple of hundred yards to the first indent in the cliff. Stay as close to the edge of the canyon as is reasonable and drop where necessary. The indent contains a constructed cattle or sheep trail. Note the steps carved into the rock. There is camping on the floor of the main canyon. (2.0–2.5 hours.)

> **Alternate route:** From the saddle on the east side of the mesa drop north down a steep slab to a thin red ledge. Follow this west until it ends. Drop to another red ledge (Class 4, 40′, lots of exposure, belay). Continue traversing west until you are near the west end of the mesa. Ascend slickrock to a level plain. To the southwest is a short and wide side canyon or bay. Descend steep slickrock to the head of this sheer-walled side canyon. See the preceding paragraph for further directions.

> **Water:** Hike up the main canyon for fifteen minutes. There

are several medium springs before the canyon boxes. A second source of water can be found by hiking down the main canyon for a couple of minutes, then hiking up the first major side canyon to the left (E) for fifteen minutes to an area of medium springs. A third source of water can be located by continuing down the North Fork for two hours to the large springs. See Day Five for details.

Day Five. 2.5 hours with backpacks. Angel Point map. There is water most of the day.

Note: This is a short day with backpacks. There is plenty of time to dayhike in the main fork of No Mans Canyon. (See the digression below.) If you do not plan to dayhike, days five and six can be combined.

Down the North Fork of No Mans Canyon

(Angel Point map.) Hike down the North Fork of No Mans Canyon. The first part is in a sandy wash and on long stretches of slickrock. The canyon narrows and becomes choked with willows in an area of large springs. (Map Seven.) The main fork of No Mans Canyon is easy to miss in all the underbrush. It comes in from the east at a fall that is ten feet above stream level. There is a large spring-fed pool at its base. (1.5–2.0 hours.)

Digression: The main fork of No Mans Canyon is worth exploring. To get into the canyon it is easiest to climb a cottonwood tree for the first ten feet. After entering the canyon, look for a cairned route to the left (LUC). It goes up the Kayenta, around a spring area that is choked with thick underbrush, and above several falls before dropping back into the canyon, which ends at a pour-off. (2.0–3.0 hours round-trip.)

Five minutes downcanyon from the confluence of the North and main forks of No Mans Canyon there is an inviting set of small falls and pools. The stream continues for another fifteen minutes and then dives underground and does not reappear. There is camping in the area. (0.5 hours.)

Water: This area has perennial springs.

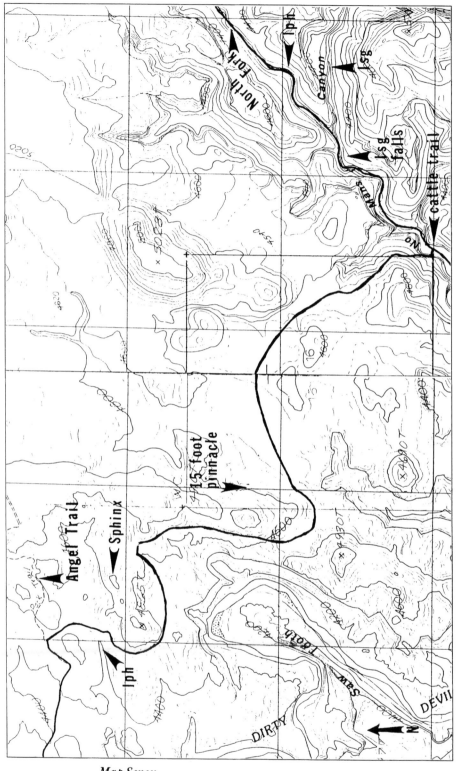

Map Seven

Day Six. 5.0 to 6.5 hours. Angel Point and Angel Cove maps. There is no reliable water along the route until the end of the day.

Exit No Mans Canyon

(**Angel Point map.**) Fifteen minutes down the canyon from the small falls look for a rubble- and boulder-filled side canyon coming in from the left (LDC)(E) (shown one-half mile southwest of elevation 5103T). Two hundred yards past it, on a wall to the right (LDC)(W), is a constructed cattle trail winding its way up a break in the Wingate.

> **Digression:** It takes twenty minutes to hike down to the Dirty Devil River from here. There are two caves along the right-hand wall that were used by Fremont Indians.

Hike up the cattle trail. At the top of the Wingate, past the first constructed portion of the cattle trail, traverse north along a Kayenta ledge for 200 yards; then ascend the short second section of constructed trail. You will end up in a short canyon with a cave on its north wall. Go northwest: up a steep hill, out of the canyon, and to the top of the Kayenta. Proceed northwest to the head of the canyon. (The drainage leading into this canyon starts southwest of elevation 5028T.) (1.0–1.5 hours.)

To the Angel Trail

From the head of the canyon continue northwest up the vague drainage. In eight minutes you will be on a flat, blackbrush-covered plain surrounded by Navajo domes. (**Angel Cove map.**) To the northwest is a long Navajo escarpment with a fifteen-foot pinnacle at its base. The pinnacle can be difficult to see. A quarter mile to the left (W) of the pinnacle is a short canyon that cuts through the escarpment (between elevation 4930T and a marked 4600-foot contour line to the north on the map).

Go west up the canyon. It comes to a dead end in a quarter of a mile. Ascend steep slickrock to the right (LUC)(N) to the top of the canyon. Continue west until you are confronted with a marvelous view of the Dirty Devil River and the Saw Tooth Ridge.

Don Murch at the spring area in No Mans Canyon.

Let the fun begin! The goal is to traverse north along the west side of a ridge. (The ridge contains elevation 4910T.) Go north up a slickrock slab until you are halfway to the top of the ridge. Traverse west, then north, across astounding slickrock. Use ledges at varying altitudes to avoid steep sections.

In fifteen minutes you will be on the rim of a small canyon. There is a white sphinx-shaped dome to the north and a larger dome to its left (W) (elevation 4865T). Skirt around the left (W) side of the larger dome. Do this by dropping southwest down the small canyon to a sandy bowl; then exit the bowl on steep slickrock to the north. Continue north, then northeast, to the north side of the dome (elevation 4865T). You will be on the rim of a V-shaped canyon with a slot at its bottom. Go down slickrock (NE) until you are in a sandy area at the head of the slot. (The slot is one-quarter mile north of elevation 4865T.)

> **Rock climber's note:** Without a pack, descend the slot. There are numerous large potholes to stem, chimney, or swim across. The slot contains two small natural bridges and ends at the edge of an impressive cliff. There are several short technical slots upcanyon as well.

From the top of the slot walk upcanyon for 100 yards until it divides. Exit the canyon by going north up a very steep, short slab to a saddle. You are now on the Angel Trail. (It is shown as a Pack Trail on the map.) Look for cairns. (2.0–2.5 hours.)

> **Digression:** To go up the Angel Trail to Angel Point, hike northwest around a dome. Cut east between this dome and the next one. There is a line of cairns between the domes. Follow them first west along the north side of a drainage, then north up a steep slab. The slab has a constructed section of trail. From the top of the slab the trail is easy to follow to the top. (1.0-hour round-trip.)

> **Historical note:** The Angel Trail was established by local ranchers in the 1870s for getting their cattle across the Dirty Devil Gorge. It was named by Cap Brown, who thought that only an angel with wings could find a way out of the canyon.

To the Dirty Devil

From the saddle stay at the present level and contour west for 200 yards on the north side of a dome. Drop off the slickrock to a small plain. The well-worn Angel Trail will be obvious. The trail is lined with many cairns. Follow them assiduously. They often do not lead the way one thinks they should. Once at the river you will see Angel Cove on the far side (W). (1.0 hour.)

> **Option:** Robbers Roost Canyon is a short distance upriver. See Option Three for notes on exploring the canyon and its tributaries.

Walk down the Dirty Devil for five minutes and cross at its confluence with Beaver Box Canyon. (This is the long, unnamed canyon coming in from the southwest one-half mile south of Angel Cove.) Although there is camping at the junction of the Dirty Devil and Beaver Box Canyon, and at Angel Cove, there is better, albeit dry, camping on the slickrock above. Day Seven is a long one; a jump-start will make things easier.

> **Digression:** For those who left a car at the top of the Angel Trail, follow a path up a prow (WSW) on the north side of the confluence of the Dirty Devil and Beaver Box Canyon. Follow a line of cairns along benches and up steep Navajo slickrock to the trailhead. This route to the top of the Navajo is often thought of as being part of the original Angel Trail. In fact, however, the Angel Trail went up Beaver Box and exited near the head of the canyon. (1.0 hour.)

Beaver Box Canyon has a perennial flow of silt-free water. There are beaver ponds a short distance up the canyon. The next reliable water source is at the trailhead. You will reach it at the end of Day Seven. Load up with water before you leave Beaver Box Canyon.

Exit the Dirty Devil

Cross to the south side of Beaver Box Canyon and go south up a sandy hillside and onto the slickrock. Above is a large dome (elevation 4620T). Go to its left (E) side. There are many route options to the top. Wind your way south-southeast up the colorful slickrock. The route is steep at times, but there should be no danger. There are many breaks and bowls that afford excellent camping with fine views of the Dirty Devil. (1.0–1.5 hours.)

> **Water:** This is a dry camp. Water will have to be carried from Beaver Box Canyon.

Day Seven. 7.5 to 8.5 hours. Angel Cove, Baking Skillet Knoll, and Burr Point maps. There is no water along the route.

To Burr Point

(**Angel Cove map.**) Continue south-southwest to the top of the cliff. Follow the rim of the Dirty Devil Gorge south. (**Baking Skillet Knoll** and **Burr Point maps.**) Tie together old mining tracks and cattle trails as you are best able. The first couple of hours provides superb views of the Dirty Devil Gorge and surrounding country. The closer you get to Burr Point the more tenuous the trails become. Stay well above the side canyons. The last couple of miles are admittedly a bit long. (7.5–8.5 hours.)

Option One. This is a direct route from Larry Canyon to No Mans Canyon. 3.0 to 5.0 hours. Angel Point map. There is no reliable water until the end of the day. When combined with Day Three, this option can reduce the trip length by one day.

Exit Larry Canyon

(**Angel Point map.**) Twenty minutes up Larry Canyon from the Dirty Devil is a less-than-vertical Wingate wall on the left (W). (If you go too far upcanyon you will intersect a side canyon that contains a large cave coming in on the right (E). Backtrack for 300 yards.) Although the wall doesn't look promising, it is only moderately difficult. However, it does have horrendous exposure. This is the only section of wall that looks possible to ascend.

To climb the wall, go back down the canyon and around the first corner to a low point on the wall. Scramble up the wall to the first bench and traverse north for 150 yards, then go up fifty feet to the next level (several possibilities). Traverse a much thinner ledge north for seventy-five yards to a low angle crack/chimney. The ledge ends here. Climb the crack (Class 4+, 50′, belay). Traverse north for twenty-five yards (Class 4, thin, lots of exposure, belay). Work up a steep slab to the top of the Wingate. Traverse north on a ledge for 200 yards until the ledge widens onto a white patio. Scramble up ledges to the northwest and squeeze up a short chimney/ramp under a chockstone. Traverse right again, then up onto the Kayenta. (1.0–1.5 hours.)

To No Mans Canyon

Proceed initially west-northwest, then north between the Navajo to the east and the Dirty Devil to the west. Always stay below the Navajo. As you near No Mans Canyon note a large tower with a small vertical arch standing at the west end of a Navajo ridge. Pay close attention to landmarks because the descent into No Mans Canyon is difficult to locate.

On the far side of the tower intersect and follow a deer trail. In five minutes, traverse around the head of a short canyon. In another ten minutes, traverse around the head of a longer, deeper canyon. In yet another ten minutes you will be on a point with No Mans Canyon below you to the left (W) and a large side canyon or bowl on the right (NE) (shown one-half mile southwest of elevation 5103T).

> **Digression:** Walk out to the point. To the northwest, across the canyon, is a constructed cattle trail winding its way up the Kayenta. This is the exit from No Mans Canyon.

Enter No Mans Canyon

Cross the top of the first small canyon that cuts through the bowl. From the rim of the second and much deeper canyon, follow the deer trail to the bottom. If you miss the trail, simply zigzag your way down Kayenta ledges. Follow the canyon into No Mans Canyon. There is some thrashing through a grove of Gambel oak. Locate the cattle trail on the far wall. (2.0–3.5 hours.)

> **Water:** There is an area of large springs, pools, and falls fifteen minutes up No Mans Canyon with good camping nearby. The Dirty Devil is a twenty-minute walk down the canyon.

Option Two. The route down the South Fork of Robbers Roost Canyon is both scenic and technically difficult. It is 9.5 to 15.0 hours to the Dirty Devil. Angel Point, Robbers Roost Flats, and Angel Cove maps. In

the South Fork there are large springs scattered along the canyon floor.

> **Warning:** This route is for rock climbers and experienced canyoneers only. It is difficult, technical, and potentially dangerous. It adds one or two days to the length of the trip. The South Fork is a tough canyon to negotiate with packs. There are five rappels that vary from ten to forty feet in length. A 100-foot rope, five slings, and ten rappel rings are necessary. Boulders, bushes, and trees can be used for anchoring the rope. Each member of the party should have a sit harness and appropriate gear for rappeling. If there are less-experienced people in the group, they should be lowered or their rappels should be belayed.

To Roost Spring

(Angel Point map.) Go north from the head of Larry Canyon. Intersect a graded road within a couple of minutes. Follow it north-northwest for forty-five minutes to a track going north. (The track goes by Lost Spring.) Follow the track for ninety minutes to the head of the South Fork of Robbers Roost Canyon. **(Robbers Roost Flats map.)** A sandy track leads west down to Roost Spring, which has a perennial flow of water. (2.5–3.0 hours.)

> **Historical note:** Roost Spring had been used for watering livestock for many years, but Cap Brown made it famous by introducing Butch Cassidy and the Wild Bunch to this remote outpost in 1884. The Wild Bunch was not a tightly knit gang; rather, it consisted of small unaffiliated bands of outlaws who used Roost Spring as a hideout after bank jobs and livestock-stealing forays. The miscreants shared the springs with local ranchers. By 1900 the West was becoming a tamer place and the Wild Bunch slowly disbanded.

Down the South Fork

Continue down the canyon. Note the cowboy glyphs on the right.

> **Historical note:** There are at least two glyphs worthy of note. Pearl Biddlecome [Baker] etched her name on the rock in March 1918. Author of *The Wild Bunch at Robbers Roost* and *Robbers Roost Recollections*, Pearl Baker lived in the Robbers Roost area from 1909 to the mid-1930s. Her

father Joe first settled the family at Roost Spring. He improved the spring and built the still-used watering trough. They later moved their cattle operation to Crow Seep, a short distance to the south.

N. [Norville] Wolverton left his name on August 19, 1912. Norville was the son of Edwin Thatcher Wolverton, who lived in the Henry Mountains from the early 1900s to the mid-1920s. He built an ore and lumber mill near the foot of Mount Pennell. Though the mill never did well, it did become a local landmark after it was moved and later restored near the BLM office in Hanksville.

The first of the five rappels is below the glyphs, down a twenty-five-foot chute. **(Angel Point map.)** There are many short obstacles, several rappels, and long stretches of tight narrows ahead. After recent rains there also may be some wading. There is a medium spring at the junction with the first side canyon coming in from the left (E) (shown one-half mile to the southwest of elevation 5348T). It is worth exploring. There is camping in the area. The last rappel is below the side canyon. (3.0–6.0 hours, depending on the size and experience of the group.)

The walking is easy along the sandy floor of the South Fork. Large springs surface from time to time and there are many good campsites. **(Angel Cove map.)** (4.0–6.0 hours.)

Water: There are several large springs in the middle and lower portions of the South Fork. Medium springs appear in the main canyon between the mouth of the South Fork and the Dirty Devil.

Option Three. Robbers Roost Canyon and its four forks are a joy to explore. Navajo walls, large springs, and exceptional narrows make these canyons popular with backpackers. It will take three to five days to explore all the forks. Angel Cove, Angel Point, and Point of Rocks East maps. There are large springs throughout this canyon system, but it is sometimes an hour or two between them.

To Robbers Roost Canyon

(**Angel Cove map.**) From the junction of the Dirty Devil and the Angel Trail go north along the river for thirty minutes to the mouth of Robbers Roost Canyon. There will be some wading. Across the river, west of the mouth of the canyon and under a large overhang, are a set of Barrier Canyon–style pictographs and several Fremont Culture petroglyphs.

Exploring the South Fork

(**Angel Cove** and **Angel Point maps.**) The South Fork joins the main canyon on the right (S) one-half hour from the river. There are occasional large springs along the canyon floor and plenty of good campsites. The canyon ends at a fall. (8.0–10.0 hours round-trip.)

Exploring White Roost

An hour and a half up the main canyon from the mouth of the South Fork note an arch high on the right-hand wall above a cliff dune (just east of the "s" in Robbers on the **Angel Point map**). You will have to look downcanyon to see it. A path under the arch provides the only easy egress from the main canyon.

It takes another forty-five minutes to reach White Roost, which comes in on the left (N). Forty minutes up White Roost is a boulder-strewn gully going up and to the left (NW). This is the only place that looks feasible to exit the canyon. The gully contains an abandoned cattle trail. (**Point of Rocks East map.**)

> **Historical note:** There are actually two cattle trails in the gully: one goes up the gully for several hundred yards before exiting onto slickrock to the right (LUC); the other traverses onto the slickrock near the mouth of the gully and ascends a couple of switchbacks carved into the rock before going up a steep dugway. At the foot of the trail is a cowboy glyph carved into the rock by John H. White on January 6, 1904. Some have wondered if White Roost was named for John H. White, but I have found no definitive answer. In a small alcove 100 yards downcanyon from the bottom of the trail, on the left (LDC), is another glyph that states:

Dog had Puppyes here—7
A.R. Weber Feb. 23, 1935
working on trail
F.E.R.A.
[Federal Emergency Relief Administration]

White Roost contains several large springs. Toward its end, the canyon divides. The left (N) fork ends in a fall. The right (E) fork tapers into a challenging set of narrows that will be of interest to rock climbers. (2.0–3.0 hours round-trip.)

Exploring the Middle Fork

(Angel Point map.) From the mouth of White Roost it takes twenty minutes to reach the junction of the North and Middle forks. The amply watered Middle Fork comes in on the right (ESE). It is wide open and spacious along its lower reaches. An hour upcanyon an area of large springs ends below a rockslide and the canyon narrows. Skirt a fall on the right (LUC). Pass a steep pour-off that drops into a medium pothole on the right (LUC) by executing a moderately difficult mantle move (Class 5.5, 8′). The canyon ends at a pour-off above a slickrock bowl. (3.5–5.0 hours round-trip.)

Exploring the North forks

(Angel Point map.) The North Fork divides in forty minutes. The main or left fork (N) is the longer canyon and has a number of enjoyable side canyons. There are large springs in the lower section of the main fork. The upper stretch is usually dry. Near the end of the canyon it divides. It is hard to tell which is the main fork. Go left (NW). The canyon ends at a short fall after first passing through a corridor-like narrows. **(Point of Rocks East map.)** (4.0–6.0 hours round-trip.)

Rock-climber's note: There is a difficult exit out of the North Fork. From the end of the canyon walk back through the corridor-like narrows. The first side canyon, a slot, enters on the right (N). The second side canyon also comes in on the right (N). This is the exit canyon (shown to the east of elevation 5163T). It is wide at its mouth but narrows after about 100 yards. After a quarter mile the canyon seems to end. Climb ten feet up a chimney, then ascend a ten-foot wall into a slot (Class 5.2). Proceed upcanyon. There are many awkward moves through tight narrows and over chockstones. (1.5–3.0 hours round-trip.)

(Angel Point map.) The right fork (NE) of the North Fork divides in twenty minutes. **(Point of Rocks East map.)** The left or main fork (N) ends in a hanging garden below an impressive cave. This is the Mind Bender Fork. The right fork (E) passes through a long stretch of large springs before it ends in an alcove. (2.0–2.5 hours round-trip.)

Exploration

Standing atop The Block high over the southern reaches of the Dirty Devil was a pivotal experience for me. Bill Booker, canyonmeister extraordinaire, had brought Harvey Halpern, Bud Evans, and me to the top of this solitary mesa one stormy fall day, desiring to show us some of the country he knew so well. Bill has spent a lifetime exploring the canyons of southern Utah and, as a resident of Hanksville, has taken every opportunity to hike the drainages of the Devil. The house of Bill and his wife Lyn has become a home away from home for canyoneers over the years, and scores of adventures have been recounted around their dinner table.

Enthralled by the view from The Block, we listened intently as Bill pointed out the salient features visible from our isolated stance: Dark Canyon, the Mille Crag Bend of the Colorado River, the Henry Mountains, Robbers Roost country, and the Capitol and San Rafael reefs. I was most intrigued by the huge expanse of the Red Benches lying beneath our feet. I had worked out a route from Happy Canyon north to Hanksville that followed the east side of the Dirty Devil and entailed no wading. The Red Benches, with luck, might be the key to a nonwading route between Happy Canyon and the mouth of the Dirty Devil to the south. If such a route was possible, and if I could tie it in with a traverse of The Block, I would have a dandy loop.

That December I embarked on an eighteen-day trip, determined to see if a route was feasible. The Moqui-step exit out the top of the West Fork of Rock Canyon onto the Red Benches was a surprise, as was the old cattle trail into Fiddler Cove Canyon. The traverse from Hatch to Happy Canyon was hampered by gluey clay—recent snows having turned the old mining track into a quagmire. I had to skirt the water-filled narrows of Happy Canyon and I unintentionally missed the exit out of the canyon near the French Spring Fork. Instead, I followed a mining track out of Happy Canyon, over the Big Ridge, and down the Flint Trail to Sunset Pass.

The Block was buried under two feet of snow as I crossed its seven-mile-long summit ridge and, with snow-plastered rock all around, I was unable to find a route off its southern prow. Backtracking to Sunset Pass, I finished the trip by again traversing the Red Benches. The trip was only a partial success; to make the route interesting, I would have to spend more time looking for shortcuts.

I picked late October to try the route again, thinking that water would be plentiful and the temperatures moderate. I was joined by Harvey Halpern, Bob Bordasch, Ginger Harmon, Larry Breed, and Bud Evans. Unfortunately, we were caught in an unseasonable heat wave, with temperatures approaching 100 degrees. The Red Benches were a throat-parching terror and the often dry middle section of Happy Canyon was spanned in the moonlight as we raced from one water source to the next. The French Spring Fork provided a welcome break from the heat and, with plenty of water available, we spent a couple of days exploring its hidden recesses. The hike from Happy Canyon over the Big Ridge and across The Block was almost our undoing: we had to carry three gallons of water apiece. However, the Block, with its sublime views and remarkable constrictions, more than made up for the hardships, and once we reached the trailhead we realized we had completed a great loop.

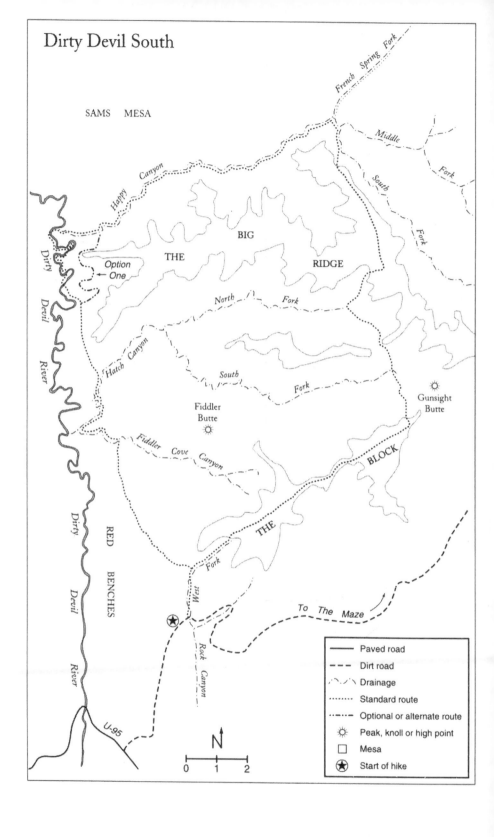

Dirty Devil South

SAMS MESA

French Spring Fork

Middle

Fork

Happy

Canyon

South

BIG

THE

RIDGE

Fork

Dirty

Option
One

North

Fork

Devil

Hatch Canyon

South

Fork

River

Fiddler
Butte

Gunsight
Butte

Fiddler Cove Canyon

BLOCK

THE

Dirty

RED

Fork

BENCHES

Devil

West

To The Maze

River

Rock Canyon

U-95

N

0   1   2

	Paved road
- - -	Dirt road
⌇⌇	Drainage
⋯⋯	Standard route
·–·–	Optional or alternate route
☼	Peak, knoll or high point
□	Mesa
✪	Start of hike

The Dirty Devil South

*It may be a characteristic of desert country that appreciation
comes most fully only after an accretion of experience, built
layer on layer through the years of a person's life.*

Ruth Kirk, 1973

**General
description:**

Diverse is the one word that best describes this hike.
From wide-open benchlands to dramatic narrows, from
mesa tops down through the walls of time, this route offers the very best to the eclectic explorer. The rarely visited Red Benches are an interesting area of Moenkopi
badlands that have been cut by small washes. They are
dominated by Fiddler Butte, a Chinle-based formation
topped by two Wingate towers. Hatch and Fiddler Cove
canyons contain a wonderland of arches, pinnacles, and
towers molded from Organ Rock Shale and crowned with
White Rim Sandstone. Happy Canyon, with its White
Rim–walled narrows, is certainly one of the most powerful
gorges in canyon country. The Block, a true island in the
sky, offers sublime hiking and far-reaching views of the
surrounding desert.

While the northern areas of the Dirty Devil River were
frequented by the Fremont Indians, the lower canyon was
a transitional area between the Fremont and the Anasazi.
Evidence of both cultures has been found there. Sheep-
herders and cattle ranchers have used the area since the
mid-1800s, and stories are told of cattle rustlers using Poison Spring and Hatch canyons to move their ill-gotten
gains across the Dirty Devil Gorge. Some of the uranium-
mining roads were constructed in the late 1950s, others in
the late 1970s.

The route begins by crossing the Red Benches and
then enters Fiddler Cove Canyon by way of an abandoned
cattle trail. A short hike up Hatch Canyon leads to an en-
ergetic exit and a long march into the inimitable narrows

of Happy Canyon. From the French Spring Fork of Happy Canyon, the route becomes much more strenuous as it goes over the Big Ridge, crosses the heads of North and South Hatch canyons and, with a vigorous scramble, ascends to the top of the north end of The Block. A steep descent off the south end of The Block leads back to the trailhead.

Trip length: Nine days minimum. Layover days, digressions, and an option can add a day or two more to the length of the trip.

Elevation range: 4530' to 7020'.

Recommended seasons: Due to the lack of water along several stretches of this hike, the recommended seasons are short: February 15 to April 1 and October 15 to December 1. **This route cannot be done safely in hot weather.**

Maps: 7.5-series USGS topographic maps: Burr Point, Clearwater Canyon, Fiddler Butte, Gordon Flats, Sewing Machine, Stair Canyon, and The Pinnacle.
Metric map: Hanksville and Hite North.

Skill level: This is an extremely strenuous hike. It is only suitable for hardcore canyoneers in top physical condition. There is difficult route finding and Class-5.1 climbing. The leader must be familiar with belay techniques and be capable of leading the climbing sections without protection. There are many places with lots of exposure. Water will be a problem; there are two or three dry camps. Read the text carefully about details concerning water before starting the trip.

Special equipment: A sixty-foot climbing rope is adequate. There are about three hours of easy wading along the Dirty Devil River, for which tennis shoes will be sufficient. Each member of the group should have the ability and capacity to carry three gallons of water.

Dirty Devil River water is just that—dirty, filthy, scummy, mucky, and yucky. A good water filter is essential.

Administering agency: Henry Mountains Resource Area, Bureau of Land Management, 406 S. 100 W. Hanksville, Utah 84734. (801-542-3461) In case of an emergency, there is a park ranger and a telephone at Hite Marina.

Land status: The west side of the Red Benches, lower Fiddler Cove Canyon, and lower Hatch Canyon are in Glen Canyon National Recreation Area. The Block is in Fiddler Butte WSA. The French Spring Fork, Main Fork, and parts of the South Fork of Happy Canyon are in the French Spring–Happy Canyon WSA. Except for a cherry-stemmed road in upper Hatch Canyon, all of the lands covered in this hike are included in the Utah Wilderness Coalition proposal for wilderness status designation.

ROAD SECTION

The road to the trailhead starts at mile 46.7 on Highway 95, the highway that runs between the town of Blanding and Hite Marina. The trailhead access road is the same one that goes to the Maze District of Canyonlands National Park. The road is unsigned, but there is a stop sign. The graded road is suitable for high clearance vehicles but may be impassable when wet. There is camping along the road. Driving time from Hite Marina is one hour.

0.0 —Mileage starts at a stop sign and the road initially goes southeast.

0.2 —Cattle guard.

0.5 —Glen Canyon National Recreation Area backcountry register.

1.8 —Good slickrock camping.

2.3 —Indistinct track to the left (NNW). It is no longer used.

2.9 —Vague mining track to the left (W). After crossing a flat area, the track cuts diagonally upward across narrow bands of Organ Rock Shale and White Rim Sandstone and tops out on the Moenkopi Formation. (The track is not shown on the **Sewing Machine map**. It starts one-quarter mile south of elevation 4508AT.) This track provides alternate access to the head of the West Fork of Rock Canyon.

Follow the track. It turns north at the Moenkopi and skirts the west rim of the West Fork of Rock Canyon. The track goes away from the rim of the canyon for a short distance, then returns to the rim near the head of the canyon. (1.5–2.0 hours.)

4.3 —Corral on the left. This is the trailhead. There is plenty of parking and room for camping. The corral is still used, so park well away from it. There is no trail register. (The corral is shown a quarter mile north of elevation 4523T on the **Sewing Machine map**.)

> **Note:** In his novel *The Monkey Wrench Gang*, Edward Abbey describes this road. It was used by Hayduke and the Monkey Wrench Gang during their attempted escape from the relentless Bishop Love after an unsuccessful attempt to blow up the White Canyon bridge.

Day One. 8.0 to 11.5 hours. Sewing Machine, Fiddler Butte, and Stair Canyon maps. There is no water until the end of the day.

> **Alternate route:** Both of the exit routes out of the West Fork of Rock Canyon are difficult. An alternate access route is available. See the Road Section at Mile 2.9 for details.

Up the West Fork of Rock Canyon
(**Sewing Machine map** and **Map Eight.**) From the corral go north into the West Fork of Rock Canyon. (The West Fork is unlabeled on the map. It is the prominent canyon to the west of the labeled Rock Canyon.)

> **Geology lesson:** You are walking on Cedar Mesa Sandstone. The fins to the right (E) are composed of brown Organ Rock Shale topped with White Rim Sandstone.

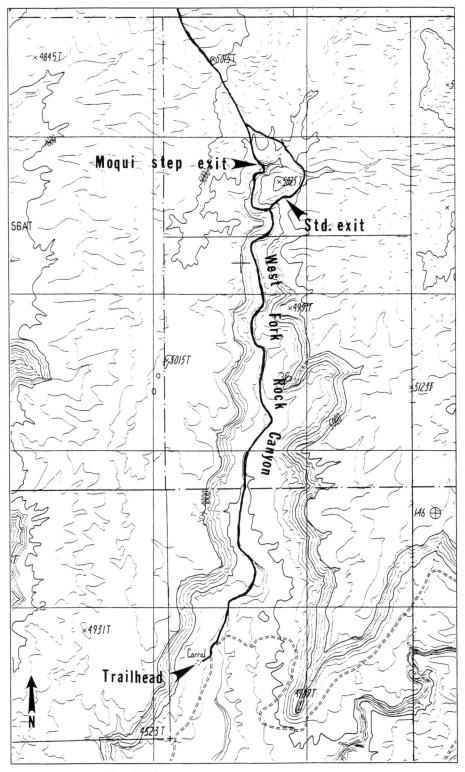

Map Eight

In forty-five minutes the canyon starts to narrow. Look for a cave with a flat top and a sloping floor on a south-facing wall to the right (LUC). The cave is at the interface between Organ Rock Shale and White Rim Sandstone and is the only large cave in the canyon. (It is immediately south of elevation 5025T.) The cave was once used by Anasazi Indians. Hike up to the cave, traverse east for 200 yards, and climb up a chimney in the White Rim Sandstone (Class 5.1, 15', belay and haul packs.) The chimney is not apparent from the canyon floor. Hike to the head of the West Fork. (1.0–1.5 hours.)

Rock-climber's note: For experienced rock climbers, there is a more adventurous exit out of the canyon. Proceed up-canyon (N) for another ten minutes until you are 150 yards from the end of the canyon. Scramble up an unlikely looking slot to the left (LUC)(W). The lower section is easy (Class 4), but you will have to lift packs from ledge to ledge. The upper section narrows considerably. Note a row of weathered Moqui steps going up the left-hand wall. This section can be climbed in a couple of steps (Class 5.5, two 35-foot pitches, belay and haul packs). There is no protection possible and there is much loose rock. Hike to the head of the canyon. (Add 1.0 hour.)

Geology lesson: You are now on the Red Benches and are in the Moenkopi Formation. To the east are the Wingate walls of the Sewing Machine and Needle, and to the northeast are the Wingate walls of The Block. The grayish slope at the foot of the vertical Wingate walls are the Chinle Formation. A steep vegetation-lined chute to the north-northeast is the descent route off of The Block.

Across the Red Benches

Your goal is to hike across the Red Benches and intersect Fiddler Cove Canyon a mile east of its confluence with the Dirty Devil. Hike north-northwest. It is best to stay closer to the Dirty Devil than to get too close to The Block. From high points you can determine your exact location on the map by noting the side canyons and bays coming up from the Dirty Devil. Always pick the route that looks easiest. No matter which route you choose, expect lots of ins and outs and ups and downs.

At the top of the cattle trail into Fidler Cove Canyon. Photo by Harvey Halpern.

In about an hour and a half Fiddler Butte comes into view to the northeast. **(Fiddler Butte map.)**

Historical note: Fiddler Butte was named for a fiddle-playing rancher who ran his sheep on The Block and along the Red Benches.

Intersect the rim of Fiddler Cove Canyon two miles to the west of the butte. **(Stair Canyon map** and **Map Nine.)** (6.0–8.0 hours.)

Digression: If you stay equidistant between the Dirty Devil River and The Block you may encounter the Chinese Trail, an old cattle trail that starts at Rock Canyon and enters the South Fork of Hatch Canyon after first passing the east side of Fiddler Butte. The trail is marked with huge cairns that bear a resemblance to Chinese pagodas. The trail, if you can stay on it, is very fast, but you intersect Fiddler Cove Canyon a couple of miles too far to the east.

Into Fiddler Cove Canyon

One nice thing about Fiddler Cove Canyon with its pinnacles, abandoned meanders, and long projecting fins is that it is easy to locate the descent route as you walk the rim. Find a long, White Rim-topped ridge with a brown Organ Rock Shale base jutting northwest into the canyon.

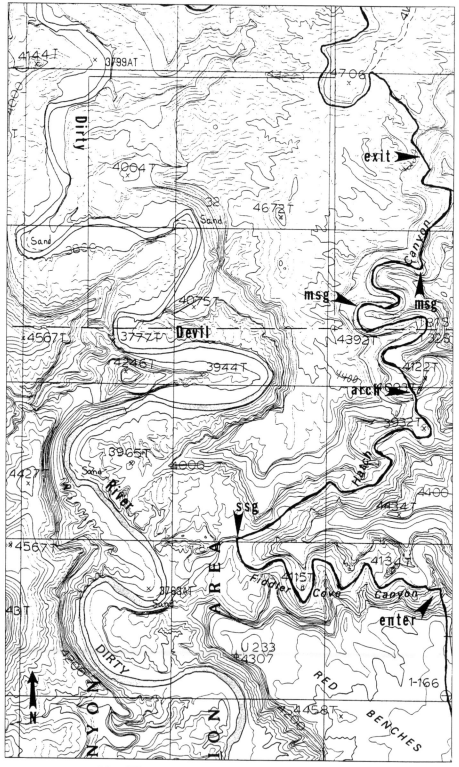

Map Nine

The ridge forces the streambed into a horseshoe-shaped bend. Downcanyon one-quarter mile is a fin-like abandoned meander (shown immediately south of the "3" and the "4" in elevation 4134T). Upcanyon from the White Rim-topped ridge is a hill with two pinnacles perched on its crest. The descent route, a steep rubble- and boulder-strewn slope, starts to the left (W) of the White Rim-topped ridge and will reveal itself as you drop. The lower portion of the route is not visible from the rim. This was formerly a cattle trail and bits and pieces of the trail are visible as you near the bottom of the slope.

Go down Fiddler Cove Canyon for a half hour to Hatch Canyon. There is camping at the confluence. You will probably spend two nights here. See Day Three for details. (1.0–2.0 hours.)

> **Water:** There is often a small flow of water at the confluence. If it is dry, continue five minutes downcanyon to the Dirty Devil River. Cattle graze in the area, so treat the water with extra care.

Day Two. This is a layover day and can be used for dayhiking in Fiddler Cove Canyon. 5.0 to 7.0 hours. There may be one hour of backpacking at the end of the day. See the text for details. Stair Canyon and Fiddler Butte maps. There is no reliable water along the route.

Dayhiking in Fiddler Cove Canyon
(Stair Canyon and **Fiddler Butte maps.)** Fiddler Cove Canyon is sinuous, serene, and surprising. The lower portion has pinnacles, short narrows, and two abandoned meanders that are interesting to scramble around. The upper portion of the canyon with its weathered Wingate walls widens for a stretch before narrowing and ending in a fantastic alcove. There are medium potholes at its head. (5.0–7.0 hours round-trip.)

> **Water:** There are two medium springs an hour up Hatch Canyon that run in springtime and after heavy rains. These are the preferred campsites since the water is clean and clear. See Day Three for details.

Pinnacles in Fiddler Cove Canyon.

Day Three. 5.5 to 7.5 hours. Stair Canyon map. There may be medium springs one hour up Hatch Canyon. If you are uncertain of this, carry water from the Dirty Devil. There is no reliable water until the end of the day.

Up Hatch Canyon

(**Stair Canyon map.**) Backpack up Hatch Canyon. Note the thin layer of Cedar Mesa Sandstone showing itself from time to time below the Organ Rock Shale. In one-half hour you pass a pinnacled fin with a vertical arch (LKA Grandma's Teapot) on its left side. (The fin is shown as elevations 4093T and 4122T.)

Twenty minutes upcanyon from the far (N) side of Grandma's Teapot is a medium spring coming from a seep on a south-facing wall. Ten minutes above this is another medium spring by a couple of large cottonwoods. There is good camping in this area. (The second spring is at the "C" in Canyon.) (1.0–1.5 hours.)

Exit Hatch Canyon

Continue upcanyon. In fifteen minutes the canyon turns from west to north, with two cottonwoods at the corner. The tree to the inside of the corner has a twisted but nearly vertical trunk; the tree closest to the creekbed

Alcove in Fiddler Cove Canyon. Photo by Harvey Halpern.

has a nearly horizontal trunk. One hundred yards past the trees the White Rim wall to the left (W) is only ten feet high. This is the start of the exit route and it is the only place that looks feasible to exit the canyon. (If you go past the exit, the canyon immediately narrows and the walls steepen.)

Ascend the ten-foot wall (Class 3+) and go up a slope to the northwest for a couple of minutes. It becomes apparent that the only way to continue up is to ascend a steep, brown slope to the west that leads to the base of a vertical Moenkopi wall. Grind your way up the slope to the base of the Moenkopi; then traverse right (N) into a shallow drainage. The traverse looks scary, but it is not technically difficult.

Continue north for one minute to the next shallow drainage and ascend it (NW) to the top. There are several easy obstacles en route. The drainage ends at an old mining track below a gray Chinle hill. (The track is shown as a 4WD road on the map. You will intersect it near elevation 4706.) (1.0–1.5 hours.)

To the Dirty Devil

Follow the mining track initially west, then north, as it parallels the Dirty Devil. In one hour Poison Spring Canyon comes into view across the river to the northwest. The track goes down a long hill. As it climbs back up, the track turns from red to yellow and, at its crest, back to red. The track "Tees" at this point; the main track goes downhill to the left (W) to the Poison Spring ford. (**Map Ten.**) Do not follow it. (1.5–2.0 hours.)

> **Digression:** The track to the Poison Spring ford of the Dirty Devil takes thirty minutes to descend. There is camping along the river.

Follow the track to the right (ENE). It is easy to miss and is not shown on the map. In eight minutes there is a "Closed to Vehicles" sign on a four-by-four post. Stay with the main track as it winds its way up a hill. The track turns sharply left (from east to north) and traverses north for five minutes before turning sharply to the right (E), toward the head of a valley. (The valley is shown to the west of elevation 4640T and an adit, which is a mine tunnel.) You will leave the track here. (If you go too far on the track, you will see some old mine shafts toward the back of the valley. They are the only mine ruins in the area. Return to the corner.) (0.5 hours.)

> **Option:** See Option One for an alternate route to Happy Canyon. This route should be used if the water in the Dirty

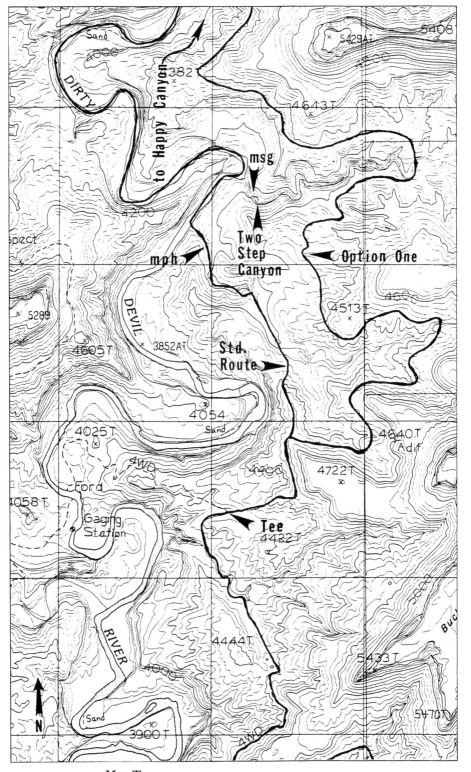

Map Ten

Devil is too high to wade. It takes several hours longer than the standard route and, due to the rough terrain, is exceptionally tiring and aggravating.

From the corner, follow a Moenkopi ridgetop initially north, then northwest, for several minutes until it is possible to drop to the valley floor to the right (N). There are many possibilities. Follow the wash down to a fall, traverse left (SW) for a couple of hundred yards, and descend a steep slope back into the canyon. The canyon narrows and there are several drops (Class 4, lower packs) to negotiate before you reach the Dirty Devil. The narrow section contains medium potholes and can be avoided by staying on the left rim.

Go up the Dirty Devil for ten minutes to the first side canyon coming in on the right (NE) (shown to the south of elevation 4643T). This is (LKA) Two Step Canyon. There is good camping on a sandy beach across the river from the mouth of the canyon. (1.5–2.0 hours.)

> **Water:** There is a medium seep 150 yards up Two Step Canyon. You can also haul water from the descent canyon if the potholes are full. If both of these sources are dry, use Dirty Devil water and treat it with extra care.

> **Rock-climber's note:** Two Step Canyon, cut in White Rim Sandstone, is both arduous to negotiate and exceptionally beautiful. There are two fifteen-foot drops to climb. Both are difficult (Class 5.6) and not only must be climbed without protection but also must be downclimbed as well. A rope and a skilled leader are essential. The farther up the canyon you go, the more amazing it becomes. (1.0–2.0 hours round-trip.)

Day Four. 5.0 to 9.0 hours. Stair Canyon, Burr Point, and The Pinnacle maps. There may be no water once you leave the Dirty Devil River. A dry camp may be necessary.

To Happy Canyon
(Stair Canyon map.) Hike up the Dirty Devil, crossing it many times, to the mouth of Happy Canyon, the

Bob Bordash climbing up Two Step Canyon.

first major drainage that enters from the right (S). (**Burr Point map.**) (2.5–4.0 hours.)

> **Note:** From this point on, and for the rest of the trip, water becomes a problem, not so much because there isn't any, but because it is in all the wrong places. Pay close attention to the text for notes on water sources. Be prepared to vary your itinerary if necessary. Always carry enough water to get

The narrows of Happy Canyon.

back to a known water source. The next reliable water source is in the French Spring Fork. You will reach it at the end of Day Five. Load up with water here.

The narrows of Happy Canyon

Hike up the fabulous narrows of Happy Canyon. Although it takes only an hour to hike through the narrows, most people will want to spend two or three hours savoring the hike and taking photographs. Near the top of the narrows there are medium potholes in the White Rim Sandstone. Exit the narrows on either side of the canyon (Class 4). (1.0–3.0 hours.)

> **Alternate route:** After recent rains, there can be chest-deep wading in the narrows. To bypass the narrows, walk five minutes up Happy Canyon from the river and ascend a steep chute (Class 3+) on the right (S). This is the only likely looking exit from the canyon. Follow the rim of the inner gorge upcanyon to the head of the narrows. (1.0–1.5 hours.)

Up Happy Canyon

The canyon widens at the top of the inner gorge and enters the Moenkopi Formation. An old mining track comes into the canyon from the right (LUC). Looking north, you will see a continuation of the track high on the hillside. Upcanyon, The Pinnacle is visible. This is the formation featured on the cover of the Utah Wilderness Coalition book *Wilderness at the Edge*.

> **Digression:** The old mining track to the north provides access to Twin Corral Box Canyon and can be used to tie this route into the Dirty Devil North hike. Scramble up the steep hillside to the track and follow it north. At times the track goes reasonably close to the river. (The track is not shown on the maps.) (5.0–7.0 hours.)

The hiking is easy along the hard-packed floor of Happy Canyon. Distances can be covered quickly. (**The Pinnacle map.**) There is a medium spring in the canyon bottom due north of The Pinnacle (one-quarter mile north of elevation 4491T). There is good camping in the area. (1.5–2.0 hours.)

> **Water:** This may be a dry camp. Water has to be hauled from the Dirty Devil River.

Day Five. 6.5 to 8.0 hours with the "Essential Digression." The Pinnacle and Gordon Flats maps. There is no reliable water until the end of the day.

To the French Spring Fork

(The Pinnacle map.) Continue upcanyon. In one hour there is another medium spring in the canyon bottom (east of elevation 4562AT). The French Spring Fork of Happy Canyon comes in on the left (N) after two more hours. **(Gordon Flats map.)** (3.0–4.0 hours.)

> **Historical note:** The French Spring Fork was named for several Frenchmen who formerly tended sheep in the area.

The route now goes up the French Spring Fork but returns to this junction on Day Seven. You can easily cache extra food and equipment by hanging it in bags from the overhanging Moenkopi cliffs.

> **Essential Digression:** You will exit the South Fork of Happy Canyon and go over the Big Ridge on Day Seven. Happily, there is a medium spring in the South Fork at the exit point. Without packs, you should check to see if this spring is running. To locate it and the exit route, continue up the Main Fork (SE) for twelve minutes to the confluence with the South Fork. Follow the South Fork (S) for fifteen minutes, passing a half-dozen fifty-five-gallon drums that are to the left (LUC). A couple of hundred yards farther up the canyon a side canyon enters from the right (S) (shown to the east of elevation 6011T). This is the exit canyon. It is the only possible route out of the canyon in this vicinity. The spring is a hundred yards farther up the main canyon. (1.0 hour round-trip.)

Up the French Spring Fork

Hike up the French Spring Fork. There is a small spring a couple of hundred yards upcanyon. After twenty minutes a large side canyon comes in from the left (N). (The canyon contains elevation 5125T on the map.)

> **Digression:** This canyon was used by ranchers to bring cattle from Twin Corral Flats into Happy Canyon. To locate the cattle trail, hike north up the canyon. Follow the main drainage, which comes out of an inner gorge onto a flat area. Follow the wash to the right (LUC)(NE). As the wash steepens, look for several large cairns to the right, above wash level. They mark the start of the constructed part of the cattle trail. If you miss them, simply continue up-

canyon to the base of a large talus slope to the right (E). A piece of the trail can be seen near the top of the slope where it enters the Kayenta. (The trail ends near elevation 6003T.) This is a worthwhile hike just to see how much work early cattlemen went through to find grazing areas for their animals. (1.5–2.5 hours round-trip.)

In case of an emergency, go north from the top of the cattle trail. In an hour you will intersect the Maze access road. The Hans Flat Ranger Station is three miles to the east.

The walking becomes a tad more difficult as you continue up the French Spring Fork. The next major side canyon comes in from the left (NW) in two hours (between elevations 6451T and 6357T).

> **Digression:** This side canyon is important because it contains a large spring twenty minutes up from its mouth. There is no camping near the spring. From the spring you can continue up to the top of the canyon. You will have to negotiate several falls (Class 5.2, 15'). (1.5–2.0 hours round-trip.)

Fifteen minutes up the main canyon is a large spring at the confluence with a small side canyon coming in on the left (N) (shown to the south of elevation 6408T). There is a pinnacle near the mouth of the side canyon and there is camping in the area. (2.5–3.0 hours.)

> **Water:** If the spring is dry, there are large potholes farther upcanyon. See Day Six for details. Use the large spring mentioned in the previous digression as a last resort.

Day Six. This is a layover day and can be used for dayhiking farther up the French Spring Fork. Gordon Flats map.

Exploring the French Spring Fork
(Gordon Flats map.) The upper end of the French Spring Fork provides excellent dayhiking. There are several falls to pass. A steep slickrock chute may be difficult to ascend when wet. Medium and large potholes dot the canyon floor. The colorful alcoves at the end of the can-

yon are a great place to relax, and one of them contains a large pool. (2.0–3.0 hours round-trip.)

> **Note:** If there was water at the foot of the exit canyon in the South Fork, you may want to camp there on the night of Day Six.

Day Seven. 5.0 to 7.5 hours. Gordon Flats map. There may be no reliable water along the route once you leave the French Spring Fork. There is a dry camp at the end of the day.

To the exit canyon

(**Gordon Flats map.**) Return to the mouth of the French Spring Fork, then to the spring at the mouth of the exit canyon in the South Fork. If you did not find water at the spring on your reconnaissance, you will have to haul water from the French Spring Fork. (2.5–3.5 hours.)

> **Warning:** Before leaving Happy Canyon, make sure your water situation has been carefully thought out. Unless there have been substantial rains within the last couple of days, you will need to carry enough water for two and a half days. The use of jump-starting techniques will help immensely. You should carry a minimum of ten quarts of water.

To the top of the Big Ridge

The exit from the South Fork to the top of the Big Ridge is visible from the canyon floor and goes up the steep slopes at the back of the side canyon. Ascend the first cliff-band by scrambling up a steep slope on the right (W) side of the canyon near its mouth. Hike to the back of the canyon. There is one minor impediment as you climb up the Wingate (Class 4). Traverse left (E) across the Kayenta to the top. (1.5–2.0 hours.)

Across the Big Ridge

Once you are on top of the Big Ridge, hike generally southeast across a gently rolling pinyon-and-juniper plain. The ridge narrows in one place, providing exciting views into the upper reaches of the South Fork of Happy Canyon. Note the Hat (elevation 6657) across the canyon to the east. There is excellent camping on the ridge. (1.0–2.0 hours.)

> **Water:** This is a dry camp. Water has to be carried from the French Spring Fork or from the spring in the South Fork.

Day Eight. 7.0 to 9.5 hours. This is a very difficult day. Gordon Flats and Clearwater Canyon maps. There is no reliable water along the route. The day ends in a dry camp.

Across the Big Ridge

(**Gordon Flats map.**) The goal is to intersect the Big Ridge road near elevation 6298T. As you get closer to the road, locate two prominent domes to the south (elevations 6363T and 6585T). Hike between the domes and drop onto the Big Ridge road. (1.0–2.0 hours.)

Go left, or generally south, on the road. (**Clearwater Canyon map.**) In fifteen minutes an often-used track branches off to the right (W). (The track is shown as a Pack Trail near elevation 6317T.) Follow it to the edge of an escarpment overlooking North Hatch Canyon to the south. There is good, albeit dry, camping on the rim.

Into North Hatch Canyon

Follow the track down the Kayenta and Wingate to the floor of the canyon. The pond shown on the map is really a stock reservoir and it is sometimes full. As the track rounds the left (E) side of a small dome (elevation 5367T) look for small potholes on the slickrock. At the floor of North Hatch Canyon the track divides. Follow the track to the left (SE) upcanyon to a pass (between elevations 6542T and 6492T). (2.5–3.0 hours.)

To the top of The Block

From the pass, Gunsight Butte in Sunset Pass is visible to the southeast and The Block is visible to the south. Your goal is to scramble 1,500 feet to the top of The Block near its north end. There are many steep talus slopes leading to the crest. All are about equal in difficulty. It is easier to pick a route from a distance than to try to find one from the base of the cliff. Though the route farthest to the north is the hardest, it does put you on top near the north end of The Block with its spectacular views, small potholes, and excellent slickrock camping. (3.5–4.5 hours.)

Water: There are small potholes in the Navajo at the north end of The Block. This is a dry camp. Water will have to be carried from the French Spring Fork or from the spring in the South Fork of Happy Canyon.

From the top of The Block you have one of the finest and most all-encompassing views in canyon country. From the east side of The Block:

North: Gunsight Butte in Sunset Pass with the Big Ridge in the background.
Northeast: The La Sal Mountains near Moab are in the background. In the foreground are the Fins in the Maze District, and the Needles District, of Canyonlands National Park.
East: The Abajo Mountains near Monticello are in the background. Just in front of them is a long ridge going to the right. This is Elk Ridge. You may be able to pick out one of the Bears Ears near Natural Bridges National Monument. Closer in towards you is the Cataract Canyon section of the Colorado River.
Southeast: Across the Colorado River is the deep, east-running Dark Canyon. Clearwater Canyon runs toward The Block. The road below goes from the trailhead to the base of the Flint Trail and into the Maze District of Canyonlands National Park.

From the west side of The Block:

North: In the very far distance are the Book Cliffs.
Northwest: Thousand Lake Mountain is in the far distance. The long white escarpment is the San Rafael Reef of the San Rafael Swell. The highest bump on the Swell is the San Rafael Knob. The thin shaft to the left of the Knob is Turkey Tower.
West-northwest: Boulder Mountain and the Aquarius Plateau are in the far distance. Capitol Reef National Park is barely visible. Factory Butte is the huge, freestanding butte.

Land bridge on top of the Block.

West: The Henry Mountains. The northernmost peak is
Mount Ellen (11,506′). In front of Mt. Ellen are the cliffs
of the Dirty Devil River.

**Day Nine. 8.5 to 11.0 hours. This is a very long day.
Clearwater Canyon, Fiddler Butte, and Sewing Machine maps. There is no reliable water along the route.**

Across The Block
(Clearwater Canyon map.) As you head southwest
across The Block, stay close to its north rim or you could
find yourself wandering along the ridge to Red Point. After two hours the ridge narrows. There is excellent camping in this area. Pass the constriction on the left (S) side
by backtracking for several hundred yards and dropping
through a short cliff-band on a constructed section of
sheep trail.

> **Historical note:** The Block was used by early sheepherders.
> Evidence of their trail-constructing handiwork is apparent in
> several places along the ridge.

After traversing under the narrow cliff-band, climb to
the top of the main ridge via an obscure chute that is just
to the left of a prow. The chute is partially blocked by pinyon and juniper trees. (2.5–3.5 hours.)

There are now two more constrictions to pass; you will walk right over the top of them. Both are narrow, dramatic, and contain evidence of an old sheep trail. The second constriction has small potholes and there is excellent camping on Navajo slickrock. (This constriction starts at elevation 6570T and ends near elevation 6668T on the **Fiddler Butte map.**) (1.0 hour.)

The top of The Block widens as you continue southwest. An old sheep and cattle trail comes in from a side canyon to the left (SE), but you will probably not be able to see it. (The trail ascends a steep canyon that is shown on the map to the south of elevation 6762T.)

> **Historical note:** As you walk along you will notice depressed areas containing innumerable flakes of chert and jasper. These lithic scatters were left behind by the Anasazi Indians who once roamed The Block. The scatters consist of chips left when the Indians flaked larger pieces of rock into arrowheads, spear points, and scrapers.

Off The Block

The descent from The Block is down a short, steep canyon that is not difficult to find; but it is hard to describe how to get there. Pay close attention to the map. As you near the south end of The Block, a dome (Orange at elevation 6803AT on the **Sewing Machine map**) can be used to help locate the descent canyon. (The descent canyon starts between "The" and "Block" on the map and contains elevation 5392AT.) (2.5–3.0 hours.)

The views from the top of the south end of The Block are impressive:

> *Southwest:* The Little Rockies. The closest summit is Mount Holmes (7,998′); the farthest summit is Mount Ellsworth (8,235′). The long ridge in the far distance is the Kaiparowits Plateau.
> *South-southwest:* The rounded summit of Navajo Mountain (10,346′).

> **Historical note:** Navajo Mountain was initially named Mount Seneca Howland by John Wesley Powell in honor of a member of his 1869 exploration party. Howland had been killed by Indians on the Shivwits Plateau near the Grand

Canyon. Almon Thompson, Powell's brother-in-law and a member of his second river expedition, later suggested renaming the peak for the Indians who lived in the area. Mount Holmes was named for W. H. Holmes, a topographer who accompanied the first surveys of the area. The Kaiparowits Plateau was called the Straight Cliffs Plateau by early settlers. Local Indians called it Kaiparowits, which means Big Mountain's Little Brother—Big Mountain referring to Navajo Mountain to the east.

Make sure you are descending the correct canyon: you should be able to see a wash going southwest from the foot of the short, steep canyon directly into the top of the West Fork of Rock Canyon. The route down the canyon through the Kayenta, Wingate, and Chinle is steep, but it is not difficult (Class 3). Before reaching the head of the West Fork, the wash goes through a Moenkopi-walled canyon and past the remnants of a huge, man-made, block-faced dam. Drop into the West Fork the same way you came. (2.5–3.5 hours.)

> **Alternate route:** Instead of dropping back into the West Fork of Rock Canyon, you can hike into the main fork of Rock Canyon. There are several descent routes near elevation 5251T. Follow the road back to the trailhead. (Add 1.0 hour.)

Option One. This alternative is much longer and has more route-finding problems than the standard route. Only the strongest hikers will make it to Happy Canyon in one day. 5.0 to 7.0 hours from the "Tee." Stair Canyon and Burr Point maps. There is no water until Happy Canyon.

To Happy Canyon

(**Stair Canyon map.**) Do not leave the track. Continue to follow it and pass over the mine workings. The track ends after another mile or so. Simply continue traversing generally north, heading many small drainages. This is hard, hard walking! On the rim of Happy Canyon (**Burr Point map**) are a series of north-pointing Moenkopi jetties that run toward the canyon. Most, but not all, will take you down to the rim of the inner gorge of

Happy Canyon. Likely candidates can be spotted from above.

> **Digression:** Instead of dropping off the jetties, you can continue traversing upcanyon at your present level. After an exceedingly difficult half mile, intersect a mining track that winds into Happy Canyon near the head of the inner gorge. (Add 0.5 hours.)

Once above the inner gorge (White Rim Sandstone), either follow the rim down to the Dirty Devil River or up to the head of the inner gorge. There is good camping at either end. See the standard route for details. (5.0–7.0 hours.)

Mountain Lions

Dark Canyon has always held a special fascination for me. One of the deepest gorges in southern Utah, its mighty walls contain a creek of incomparable beauty replete with miles of waterfalls and crystal-clear plunge pools. I have never had to wonder why the Anasazi Indians came to this place; its gentle ambience and the warmth of its dark rocks must have made it seem a Shangri-la.

The first white men known to have visited Dark Canyon were members of John Wesley Powell's second expedition in 1871. Frederick Dellenbaugh, a topographer on that trip, wrote: "It was dinner-time when we got the boats below to a safe cove, and we were quite ready for a meal which Andy meanwhile had been cooking. A beautiful little brook came down a narrow canyon [Dark Canyon] on the left, and it was up this stream the Major [Powell] went. The Major went for a mile and a half and then climbed the side. They were obliged to give it up and come back to the bottom. By this time it was too late to make another attempt, so they turned their backs on 'Failure Creek,'. . ."

Stephen Vandiver Jones, the assistant topographer, wrote in his diary, "The cañon was grand beyond description, very narrow; the walls rose almost precipitous for 2500 or 3000 feet, in a few places a talus for 300 or 400 feet, but usually very steep. A small stream rippled down through the center, broken into innumerable little cascades in places forming deep clear pools with rocky bottoms."

Equally attractive, but less well known than Dark Canyon, is Bowdie Canyon to the north. Its several forks show evidence of prehistoric occupation, and a natural bridge and an arch add texture to its already amazing aspect. The two canyons are connected by the Cataract Canyon portion of the Colorado River.

I was eager to see if I could follow ledge systems high above the Colorado River between Dark and Bowdie canyons. With a three-week supply of food on my back, I descended the Sundance Trail and hiked down Dark Canyon. I found a route that took me partway out of the canyon to a series of broken ledges and steep slopes which led to a platform some 700 feet above the river. More ledges led upcanyon. The going was rough and I cursed my heavy pack.

At one point, the ledge narrowed considerably and the way was blocked by a wall of rocks. With some effort, I pushed the rocks over the edge of the precipice and, with the use of a rope, managed to crawl across the narrow portion of the ledge. Only after succeeding trips to the area did I come to realize that the wall of rocks had certainly been man-made. Arrowheads and pottery shards found along the route revealed that this was an ancient path used by the Anasazi.

The ledge system eventually led into a canyon midway between Dark and Bowdie canyons. Although I tried to continue the above-river traverse to Bowdie Canyon, the ledge system became too tenuous and I gave up. Instead, I hiked over Middle Point and dropped into the center section of Bowdie Canyon.

The first snow of the year fell while I was exploring Bowdie Canyon. Early one morning I set off on a dayhike to investigate a couple of short side canyons. A breeze, the rustling of yellowing cottonwood leaves, and the muffling effect of freshly fallen snow underfoot allowed me to inadvertently encounter three mountain lion cubs as they frolicked in a tangle of brush and downed cottonwoods. The lioness sat nearby as her offspring played. I watch enthralled for twenty minutes, afraid to move. Finally, a shift in the wind carried my scent to the lioness and, with nary a backwards glance, the four cats vanished.

Dark Canyon

*I am not so sure whether anyone who has wandered [the can-
yon country] and looked upon the wonders that nature has
wrought—its gorges, its canyons, its mountains and its painted
rocks, and upon its ancient stone cities, and the cliff dwellings
of its canyons—is ever afterwards Quite Sane.*
Colonel Charles D. Poston, 1920

**General
description:**
Dark Canyon Primitive Area is sandwiched between Lake
Powell to the south and the Needles District of Canyonlands National Park to the north. The beauty of the area
was recognized early on and the "Primitive Area" designation has saved it from many of the ravages of development
so common in other canyon areas.

Dark Canyon starts at 8700 feet on Elk Ridge near
the Bears Ears north of Natural Bridges National Monument. In its thirty-mile course to the Colorado River,
Dark Canyon drops 5,000 feet and changes from a pon-
derosa-pine-studded highland with alpine wildflowers to a
dry sage, pinyon, and juniper desert. The canyon itself var-
ies from a U-shaped valley at its upper end to a tortuous
and narrow cleft near the Colorado River.

While the Dark Canyon drainage and its major side
canyons—Woodenshoe and Peavine—are usually busy during the hiking season, other parts of the Primitive Area
generally are left alone. The route described herein visits
the best parts of Dark Canyon and takes you to places that
may be visited by only a handful of parties a year.

Dark Canyon was first inhabited by the Anasazi Indians. Before their retreat to the south in the early 1300s,
they built the many cliff dwellings and granaries found in
Dark Canyon and in all its tributaries as well as in Bowdie
Canyon to the north. Early Mormon cattle ranchers
grazed their animals on the plateaus above Dark Canyon
and herded them down Woodenshoe and Peavine canyons
to feed on the fertile floor of the valley. The Sundance
Trail, which provides easy access to the lower end of Dark
Canyon, was also constructed by the pioneer ranchers.

The route starts high on a plateau near the conflu-

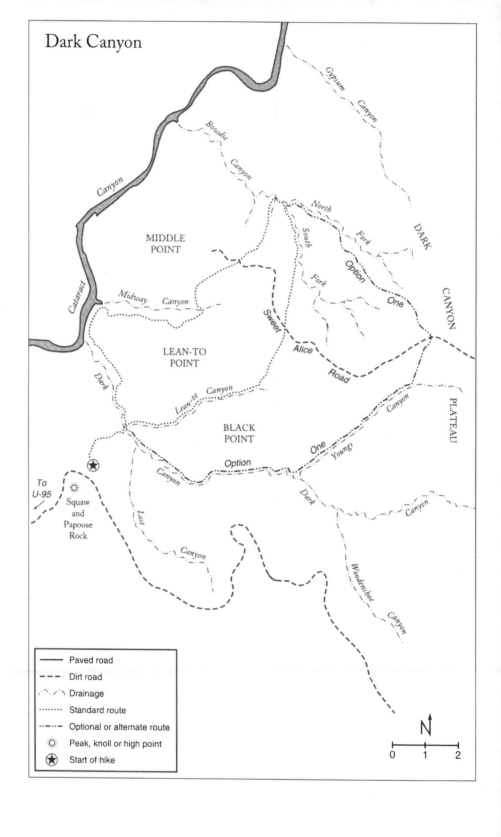

Dark Canyon

ence of Dark Canyon and the Cataract Canyon portion of the Colorado River. Using the Sundance Trail, the route drops 1,400 feet into Dark Canyon, quickly exits, and then follows a thrilling series of ledges high above Cataract Canyon along an old Anasazi route into Midway Canyon (AN). It then goes over Middle Point and into Bowdie Canyon. Two options are presented for returning to Dark Canyon: the shorter version descends Lean-to Canyon; the longer version goes down Youngs Canyon.

Trip length: Six days minimum. One day should be added to allow time to explore Bowdie Canyon or to make up for time lost on other parts of the route. Layover days, digressions, and an option can add another couple of days.

Elevation range: 3800′ to 6800′.

Recommended seasons: February 15 to April 15 and September 15 to December 1. **Due to a lack of water along several sections of this route, do not attempt this hike in hot weather.**

Maps: 7.5-series USGS topographic maps: Black Steer Canyon, Bowdie Canyon East, Bowdie Canyon West, and Indian Head Pass.
Metric map: Hite Crossing.

Skill level: This is an exceedingly demanding route and is not suitable for novices or for those out of shape. The first two days will challenge the most intrepid backpacker. There is difficult route finding and Class-5.0 climbing. The leader must be familiar with belay techniques and be capable of leading the climbing sections without protection. There are many places with lots of exposure. Water can be a problem; there are two dry camps. Read the text carefully about details concerning water before starting the trip.

Special equipment: Two ropes are essential: one fifty feet long, the other eighty feet long. Each hiker should have a minimum water capacity of two gallons. There is no wading on this trip.

Notes: Although much of this country has little traffic, Dark Canyon is becoming impacted by careless hikers. If your itinerary allows, do not camp near the foot of the Sundance Trail or at the confluences of Dark Canyon and Lean-to or Youngs canyons. Please carry out your toilet paper when in Dark Canyon. Camp fires are allowed, but it is unconscionable to use them.

Administering agencies:

San Juan Resource Area. Bureau of Land Management, 435 N. Main, Monticello, Utah 84535. (801-587-2141) Glen Canyon National Recreation Area. P.O. Box 1507, Page, Arizona 86040 (602-645-2471). Twenty-four-hour dispatch: 602-645-8883. Emergency assistance: 602-684-2242. In case of an emergency, there is a park ranger and a telephone at Hite Marina.

Land status:

The Sundance Trail and Bowdie, Lean-to, and Youngs canyons are in the Dark Canyon Primitive Area. The primitive area classification, an administrative designation given to the area in 1970 by the BLM, provides interim protection until the wilderness issue is decided by Congress. The Primitive Area is in the Dark Canyon WSA. The benchlands between the canyons covered in the hike—Dark Canyon Plateau and Middle Point—have been left out of the BLM's wilderness proposal; however, all of the lands included in this hike are in the Utah Wilderness Coalition's proposal for wilderness designation. The portion of Dark Canyon below the mouth of Lean-to Canyon and areas near the Colorado River are in the Glen Canyon National Recreation Area.

ROAD SECTION

Access to the Sundance trailhead is via county road 208A. This unsigned road starts at mile 53.3 on Highway 95, the highway running between the town of Blanding and Hite Marina. The graded road is suitable for high-clearance vehicles but may be impassable when wet. There is camping on spur roads. Driving time from Hite Marina is one hour.

0.0	—Mileage starts at the cattle guard and goes northeast.
1.1	—Glen Canyon National Recreation Area boundary sign.
4.6	—Top of a pass.

Geology lesson: The white slickrock you have been driving over is Cedar Mesa Sandstone. The brown formation you are in now is Organ Rock Shale. Look at the cliff to the east. The Organ Rock Shale goes up to a thin white band of White Rim Sandstone. The uppermost stratum, which looks somewhat like the layers of a dark chocolate torte cake, is the Moenkopi Formation. In the distance, to the north, are the vertical Wingate cliffs of The Block, the Sewing Machine, and the Big Ridge. The Cedar Mesa cliffs below are the walls of the Narrow Canyon section of the Colorado River as it makes Mille Crag Bend.

Historical note: John Wesley Powell named Mille Crag Bend for its many pinnacles and towers. Mille is Latin for thousand.

4.7	—"Y." Go right (NE).
7.0	—"Y." Go left (NE).
7.7	—"Y." Go right (E).
7.9	—In and out of a shallow canyon. Water troughs to the right.
8.0	—"Tee." Track comes in on the right. Stay with the main road to the left (NE).
8.9	—"Y." Go left (NE). The pinnacle to the left of a small butte is Squaw and Papoose Rock.
9.5	—"Tee." Track comes in on the left. Stay with the main road to the right (NE).
11.1	—"Tee." Track comes in on the left (N). Follow it. You are due north of Squaw and Papoose Rock.

11.3 | —Sundance trailhead. There is a trail register. There is plenty of parking and room for camping. (The trailhead is located at the end of a track one-half mile north-north-west of Squaw and Papoose Rock on the **Indian Head Pass map.**)

Day One. 5.5 to 7.5 hours. Indian Head Pass and Bowdie Canyon West maps. There is a perennial stream in Dark Canyon. The day ends at a dry camp.

The Sundance Trail

(**Indian Head Pass map** and **Map Eleven.**) From the register box cross the dam of a stock pond and follow the Sundance Trail northeast. The path is obvious in sandy areas and is adequately cairned as it crosses slickrock and descends several short Cedar Mesa cliffs to the edge of Dark Canyon.

> **Geology lesson:** This is a good place to get your bearings and to view the three major geologic formations visible in Dark Canyon. You are standing on the top of a vertical white cliff that is streaked with black varnish. This is Cedar Mesa Sandstone. The ledgy, slope-forming, red-and-white cliffs below the Cedar Mesa Sandstone are lower Cutler beds, which consist of both sandstone and limestone layers. The lowest cliffs, which form the inner gorge of Dark Canyon, are in the upper member of the Hermosa Formation. They consist of interwoven gray, greenish, and nearly black limestone, sandstone, and shale strata.

The trail becomes steeper and the cliffs higher and more difficult to negotiate. After dropping several hundred feet, the trail cuts right (SW) along a broken ledge to the top of an appallingly long, steep talus slope. Descend this into a short side canyon and follow it down to Dark Canyon. Aching thighs and injured knees are not unknown here! The stream has a perennial flow of water. (2.5–3.0 hours.)

Down Dark Canyon

Go down the canyon. Lean-to Canyon comes in on the right (E) in five minutes.

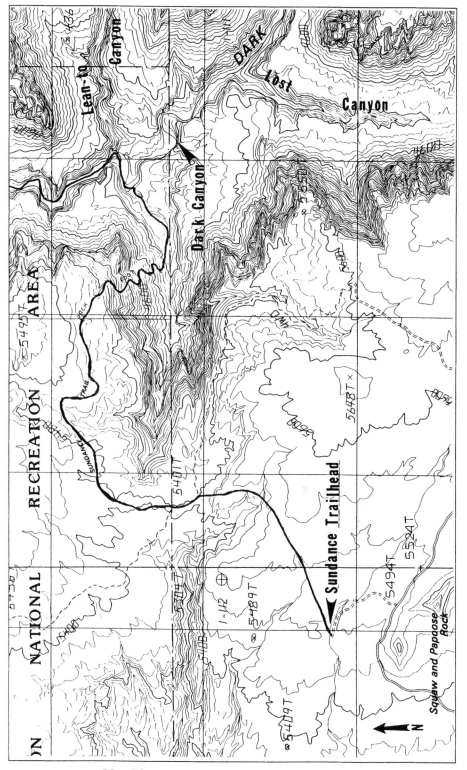

Map Eleven

Dark Canyon, near the foot of the Sundance Trail.

Digression: There is a pleasant dayhike that goes up the bottom of Lean-to Canyon to the foot of a huge fall. (1.0 hour round-trip.) To get into the upper reaches of Lean-to Canyon, locate a path that goes up a steep hillside on the right side of the canyon (LUC)(S). The path goes to the top of the aforementioned fall and to the spring-fed pools above it. (2.5–3.0 hours round-trip.)

Dark Canyon narrows and large pools and small falls line the gorge. They are in the gray/black limestones of the upper member of the Hermosa Formation. In thirty minutes you pass a narrow area by ascending a short wall on the right (Class 4, 10′). Follow a path along the rim of the narrows for twenty minutes to the mouth of a steep canyon coming in from the right (E). **(Bowdie Canyon West map.)** This is the exit canyon (shown to the north of elevation 5574T). **(Map Twelve.)** The path descends a steep slope to the canyon bottom. The gray limestone ledges contain reddish deposits of chert and jasper. (1.0 hour.)

Note: Exceptionally strong groups may wish to spend the night here, but Day Two is extremely long and difficult. A jump-start is usually in order. Day Two is a dry day. Make sure to carry plenty of water. The next reliable water source is in Midway Canyon at the end of Day Two.

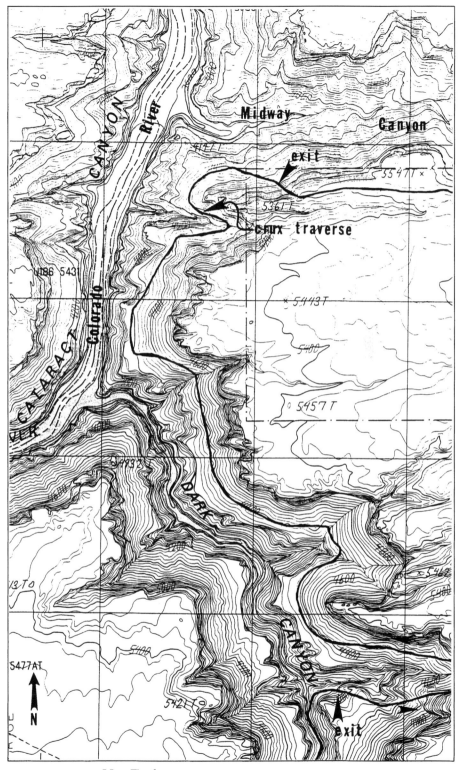

Map Twelve

Digression: The Colorado River is another thirty minutes down the canyon. There are huge swim pools and fabulous waterfalls throughout this stretch.

Exit Dark Canyon

Look up at the mouth of the side canyon to the east. A notch is visible in the wall to the right. Do not go up the floor of the canyon. Instead, ascend steep slopes and crumbly ledges through the notch to the top of the first cliff-band. Continue up steep slopes and cliffs for a long distance until you can head the side canyon. Scramble down to a wide terrace on the edge of Dark Canyon. There is superb camping on the terrace. (2.0–3.5 hours.)

Water: This is a dry camp. Water has to be hauled from Dark Canyon.

Day Two. 7.0 to 10.5 hours. Bowdie Canyon West map. There is no reliable water along the route until the end of the day.

Cataract Canyon traverse

(Bowdie Canyon West map.) Continue traversing above Dark Canyon toward Cataract Canyon. You will have to struggle across talus slopes and over boulders in places. As a rule, do not stay high; always seek the easiest path, even if it means dropping several hundred feet to likely looking benches. A terrace at the confluence of Dark Canyon and Cataract Canyon provides a welcome rest spot. (2.0–2.5 hard hours.)

Historical note: Cataract Canyon was named by members of John Wesley Powell's second expedition down the Colorado River in 1871. They felt that the ferocity of the water plummeting through this section of the canyon dictated the need for a more superlative descriptive term than "rapid." They decided on "cataract."

In 1911 Ellsworth Kolb and his brother Emery ran Cataract Canyon in small wooden boats. After the trip they wrote: "In Cataract Canyon's 41 miles there are 45 bad rapids, and there must have been at least that many men who have attempted its passage and were never heard from

The traverse ledge high above Cataract Canyon.

again." The rapids in the lower portion of Cataract Canyon have been inundated by the waters of Lake Powell.

The route continues north along talus slopes and ledges. It heads one short side canyon without problems. The next side canyon (shown to the south of elevation 5361T) contains the crux of the hike.

The crux

After heading the canyon, drop to a narrow ledge. At one point you will have to crawl under an overhanging protuberance on a three-foot-wide ledge with a 100-foot drop below it (Class 5.0, 50'). First reconnoiter this section without packs. Though not difficult, the exposure makes the crux an anxious undertaking.

There are many ways to make this passage more safe. It is imperative that everyone be belayed across the narrow ledge from both sides. On the near side, a rope can be anchored to a large boulder; the other rope on the far side can be tied around a large buffaloberry bush. Packs will have to be handed around the crux. Pack handlers should be belayed. Do not try to cross the ledge with a pack!

Historical note: In 1895 John Wesley Powell wrote: "It is curious how a little obstacle becomes a great obstruction when a misstep would land a man in the bottom of a deep chasm. Climbing the face of a cliff, a man will without hesitating walk along a step or shelf but a few inches wide if the landing is but ten feet below, but if the foot of the cliff is a thousand feet down he will prefer to crawl along the shelf." Amen.

Exit the canyon

Round a corner into Midway Canyon and immediately start working your way diagonally up short cliffbands. (Midway Canyon is not named on the map; it is the long canyon shown to the north of elevation 5547T.) Aim for the only break in the Cedar Mesa wall to the south. From below, the route is not apparent. At the base of the Cedar Mesa locate a ledge system running southeast up the wall in steep steps. (If you go too far along the base of the Cedar Mesa wall you will reach an area of recent rockfall. Backtrack for a quarter mile.) This ledge system is used by bighorn sheep and was used by the Anasazi. Look for a vertical prow with a crack running down its southwest face near the top of the cliff. Ascend a steep, loose gully containing several pinyon pines that is to the left of the prow. (The prow is immediately north of the "T" in elevation 5361T.)

From the top of the gully traverse left (E) on a ledge for several hundred yards to the first practical exit to the rim of the canyon—a steep, blocky wall (Class 4, 25′). (2.5–5.0 hours, depending on how long it takes to navigate the crux.)

Into Midway Canyon

You are now on a peninsula between Midway Canyon to the north and a short canyon to the south (shown to the south of elevation 5361T). The hiking becomes much easier. Follow the peninsula east. The canyon to the south ends. Continue east along the rim of Midway Canyon. After going around the top of a short side canyon (shown one-quarter mile west of elevation 5795T), go back to the edge of Midway Canyon and continue east. (**Map Thirteen.**) Look for a pinnacle with a large round base near the bottom of the far (N) side of Midway Canyon. The pinnacle is called The Cobra (AN). (It is shown one-quar-

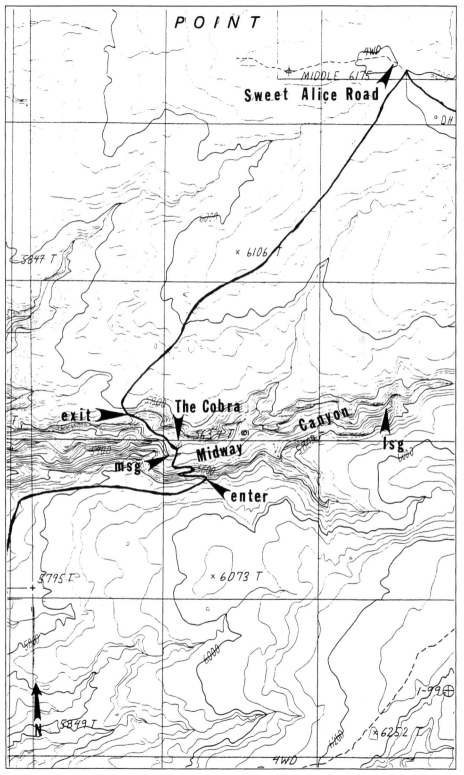

Map Thirteen

ter mile west of elevation 5634T). The pinnacle is above a thirty-foot fall. The canyon floor above the fall is flat and sandy.

The descent into Midway Canyon starts one-quarter mile east of The Cobra and descends a steep series of ledges. Some of the traverses between cliff-bands are up to a quarter of a mile long. The route is not difficult, but it is time-consuming. The final drop is down a nearly vertical chute opposite The Cobra (Class 4+, 20', belay and lower packs). There is excellent camping in this pretty Cedar Mesa–walled canyon. (2.5–3.0 hours.)

> **Water:** If water is not running in the canyon, look for a medium spring below the thirty-foot fall. There is a large spring and large potholes twenty minutes up the canyon near its head.

Day Three. 4.0 to 6.0 hours. Bowdie Canyon West and Bowdie Canyon East maps. There is no reliable water along the route until the end of the day.

Exit Midway Canyon

(Bowdie Canyon West map.) To locate the exit, hike for five minutes down the right (LDC) side of the canyon on a wide ledge past the base of The Cobra and above the fall. Look for a steep chute going west up the Cedar Mesa wall to the right (N). The chute looks improbable from the canyon floor. It is a steep (Class 3) scramble to the top.

Strike a compass course northeast (past elevation 6106T) to a 4WD track on top of a gentle ridge (Middle Point). This is the Sweet Alice road (county road 221). (1.5–2.0 hours.)

> **Historical note:** The road was named for a certain Alice, a young Indian woman who was reputed to have entertained cowboys, miners, and other male visitors while living at what is now known as Sweet Alice Spring at the top of Fable Valley, a canyon to the northeast.
>
> In his western adventure *Dark Canyon*, Louis L'Amour wrote: "As they drew up, the low wall of the aspen and pine-clad Sweet Alice Hills [to the north of Dark Canyon] was behind them, cutting them off from the view to the east.

Westward the land was afire . . . the pinks and reds of the fantastic rock formations to the west and north were weirdly lit by the dull red fire of the setting sun, while the dark fingers of the canyon that clawed toward the Colorado [Dark Canyon] were simply black streaks through the canyon."

Into Bowdie Canyon

From the road, a drainage is visible to the northeast. (The drainage is north of elevation 5982T on the **Bowdie Canyon East map.**) The route circles over the top of the drainage and goes by elevation 6060T and between elevations 6012T and 5837T. It is easiest to hike east along the road for thirty minutes; then go north. (**Map Fourteen.**) The first cliff-bands present few obstacles as you descend into a slickrock-lined bowl and along the east edge of a deep canyon.

From the rim of Bowdie Canyon locate an elongated, S-shaped ridge jutting north-northeast deep in the canyon (elevation 5564T). (Do not mistake this ridge for a similar looking but straight ridge that is downcanyon to the left [NW].) Descend cliffs to the southeast for several hundred feet toward another side drainage; then negotiate several more cliffs until you are in a saddle between the main cliff and the beginning of the S-shaped ridge. Work down the right (E) side of the ridge and into Dark Canyon. There are many choices (Class 3+). There is good camping throughout the canyon. (2.5–4.0 hours.)

> **Historical note:** The discovery and naming of Bowdie Canyon is a mystery. Stephen Vandiver Jones made an oblique reference to the narrow canyons located between Clearwater Canyon and Dark Canyon. In his diary entry of September 27, 1871, he wrote: "Many narrow deep gulches were worn to the river on the route of this day's run, some ending in the cliff wall, others winding out of sight. Very little vegetation along the banks, occasionally a few willows, sometimes a lone hackberry. Walls of mixed sand and limestone, capped either with red or gray." The two largest gulches along this stretch of river were the then-unnamed Bowdie and Midway canyons.

> **Water:** This section of canyon has a perennial stream.

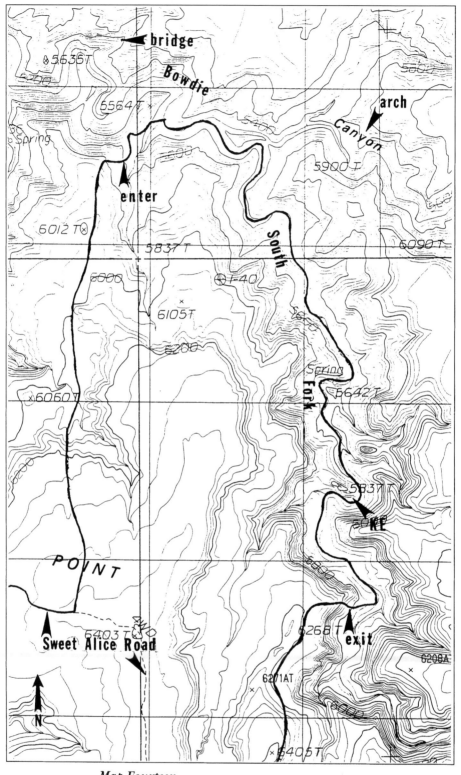

Map Fourteen

Rock-climber's note: There is a splendid route that goes down Bowdie Canyon to the Colorado River. It is difficult and technical. Bring a fifty-foot rope. Water is available in many places. The hard part is near the river, so less technically inclined adventurers can still enjoy most of the hike.

Pass the first fall on the right (LDC) (Class 5.0, 12'). The second major fall can be passed on either side by following ledges and crossing arduous talus slopes. The final fall is passed by climbing down a difficult wall (Class 5.6, 15', no protection possible) on the left. (6.0–7.0 hours round-trip.)

Day Four. 3.0 to 4.0 hours with backpacks. Bowdie Canyon East map. There is water in the South Fork of Bowdie Canyon. The day ends in a dry camp.

Note: This is a short day with backpacks. There is plenty of time to dayhike in the North Fork, explore Anasazi ruins, visit a natural arch, and enjoy the occasional pool. See Option One—Alternate Day Four (page 137) for details on exploring the North Fork.

Option: See Option One—Alternate Days Four through Seven (pp. 137, 140, 142, 143) for a longer route that exits the North Fork of Bowdie Canyon and descends Youngs Canyon back into Dark Canyon.

South Fork of Bowdie Canyon

(Bowdie Canyon East map.) Hike up Bowdie Canyon for ten minutes until it divides. The main (or North) fork is to the left (NE). Go right (SE) into the South Fork. After a half hour there is a large spring area with the necessary attendant thrashing through reeds and willows. In another half hour the canyon goes left (SE) around an abandoned meander (elevation 5837T). Before the meander, a slickrock area makes an ideal place to have dinner. Since there is a dry camp ahead, stock up with water here. The next reliable water source is in Lean-to Canyon at the end of Day Five. (1.0–1.5 hours.)

Exit the South Fork

As you pass under the south side of the abandoned meander, note the initials KE blasted with a rifle on the varnished, south-facing wall. Pay close attention to the details for finding the exit route out of the canyon. Fifteen minutes past the KE the canyon turns right (SW). The buttress at the corner (on the right) has a tiny window near its top. Hike just past the buttress and immediately ascend a steep slope to the southeast. Above the slope find a route up a broken wall. There are many choices (Class 3 to Class 4-).

Once on top of the cliff, go south. Stay on a terrace on the left (E) side of the white, summit-ridge cliffs (past elevations 6268T and 6271AT). As the terrace narrows (near elevation 6405T) there is an area of flat slickrock that is ideal for camping. (2.0–2.5 hours.)

> **Water:** This is a dry camp. Water has to be hauled from the spring area near the KE initials.

Day Five. 5.5 to 8.5 hours. Bowdie Canyon East, Black Steer Canyon, and Indian Head Pass maps. There is water in Lean-to Canyon. There is water at the end of the day.

To Lean-to Canyon

(**Bowdie Canyon East map.**) Travel south through the final cliff-band and continue south to a 4WD track. Follow the track southeast for twenty minutes to a landing strip (shown on the map at elevation 6648T). It is fifty yards to the right (S) of the road and is hard to see. Look for a six-foot post on the right and an indistinct track cutting to the runway. You are once again on the Sweet Alice road. (1.0–1.5 hours.)

The views from the landing strip are exceptional. To the:

> *Northeast:* The La Sal mountains near Moab are in the far distance.
> *North-northeast:* The elongated mesa in the background is the Island in the Sky section of Canyonlands National Park.
> *North:* The white sandstone plain is the Maze District of Canyonlands National Park.
> *North-northwest:* The Big Ridge. The Flint Trail is out of sight around the corner.

Airstrip on top of Middle Point. Henry Mountains in the background.

Northwest: The Wingate-walled mesa is The Block. The Block and the Big Ridge to its right are divided by Sunset Pass. The Sewing Machine and Needle complex is on the far left side of The Block.

West-northwest: The three major peaks of the Henry Mountains are, from right to left: Mt. Ellen (11,506′), Mt. Pennell (11,132′), and Mt. Hillers (10,737′).

West-southwest: The Little Rockies. The peak to the right is Mt. Holmes (7,998′); the one to the left is Mt. Ellsworth (8,235′).

West: The Kaiparowits Plateau is in the far distance.

South-southwest: The rounded top of Navajo Mountain (10,346′) is barely visible.

Historical note: Frederick Dellenbaugh and John Wesley Powell climbed from the Colorado River to Dark Canyon Plateau, an area to the northeast of the landing strip. From Dark Canyon Plateau, Dellenbaugh wrote: "The view in all directions was beyond words to describe. Mountains and mountains, canyons, cliffs, pinnacles, buttes surrounded us as far as we could see, and the range was extensive."

Mount Pennell was named for Joseph Pennell, an artist on several early surveys of the country. Mount Hillers was named for Jack Hillers, a photographer on the second Powell expedition.

Down Lean-to Canyon

There are many routes into Lean-to Canyon. None is hard, but all require time to find ways around drops and down bands of cliffs. To get started, go south from the landing strip to a southwest-running drainage (shown one-quarter mile southeast of elevation 6298T). Descend its right (LDC)(NW) side into Lean-to Canyon. Some scouting may be necessary. (1.5–2.5 hours.)

> **Alternate route:** There is a longer and more rewarding route that drops into the very top of Lean-to Canyon. From the landing strip continue southeast along the Sweet Alice road for twenty minutes. Leave the road (near elevation 6788T) and cut south-southwest to the edge of a cliff above a large bowl. Drop south-southwest into the bowl to a shallow drainage. This is shown as the main fork of Lean-to Canyon on the map. (Do not go all the way across the bowl or you will enter the wrong drainage.)
>
> Proceed down the canyon. There are four drops to negotiate before you join the standard route. A couple of them may take some scouting. Note the long tunnel-like natural bridge between two of the falls. The lower falls have medium springs at their bases. (Add 1.5–2.0 hours.)

> **Historical note:** Lean-to Canyon was named for a structure built at its mouth that was used by local sheep and cattle ranchers. The lean-to no longer exists.

Lean-to Canyon contains many small obstacles. Routes around the shorter falls are easy to spot. Pass the first large fall on a trail to the left (LDC). Below the fall there is usually water in an idyllic pool surrounded by red slickrock. A short distance below the fall you enter the top of a large spring area. This is the first reliable water for the day. (You go off the **Bowdie Canyon East map** and onto the **Black Steer Canyon map** for a very short distance, then onto the **Indian Head Pass map.** The spring is labeled on the **Indian Head Pass map.**) (1.5–2.5 hours.)

The spring area is troublesome—a real bear. Past it the canyon floor becomes slickrock. There are occasional pools and small falls. Reach a huge U-shaped fall. There is excellent camping throughout the area. (1.5–2.0 hours.)

Water: There is usually water flowing down to the U-shaped fall. If the fall is dry, carry water the short distance from the bottom of the spring area or continue hiking for one hour to Dark Canyon.

Day Six. 3.5 to 5.0 hours. Indian Head Pass map. There is a perennial flow of water in Dark Canyon.

To Dark Canyon

(Indian Head Pass map.) Pass the U-shaped fall on an established and cairned trail to the left (LDC). It leads into Dark Canyon. (1.0–1.5 hours.)

To the trailhead

Ascend the Sundance Trail back to the start. At least the packs are now light and your legs should be in shape. (2.5–3.5 hours.)

Option One—Alternate Day Four. This option adds one day to the length of the trip. The route goes out the North Fork of Bowdie Canyon and down Youngs Canyon into Dark Canyon. 3.5 to 4.5 hours with backpacks. Bowdie Canyon East map. There is water throughout the North Fork of Bowdie Canyon. There is a dry camp at the end of the day.

Note: This is a short day with backpacks. There is plenty of time to dayhike in the South Fork and explore Anasazi ruins. See Day Four for details.

North Fork of Bowdie Canyon

(Bowdie Canyon East map.) Hike up Bowdie Canyon for ten minutes until it divides. The South Fork is to the right (SE). Go left (NE) up the North Fork. After twenty-five minutes note the large arch high on a wall to the left. In another hour the canyon divides at a spring area (shown to the west of elevation 5940T). **(Map Fifteen.)** Go right (S). After twenty minutes a short canyon comes in on the right (S) (shown one-quarter mile east of elevation 6455T). This is the exit canyon.

If you are in no rush, continue up the canyon for another ten minutes to an area of slickrock. This area is

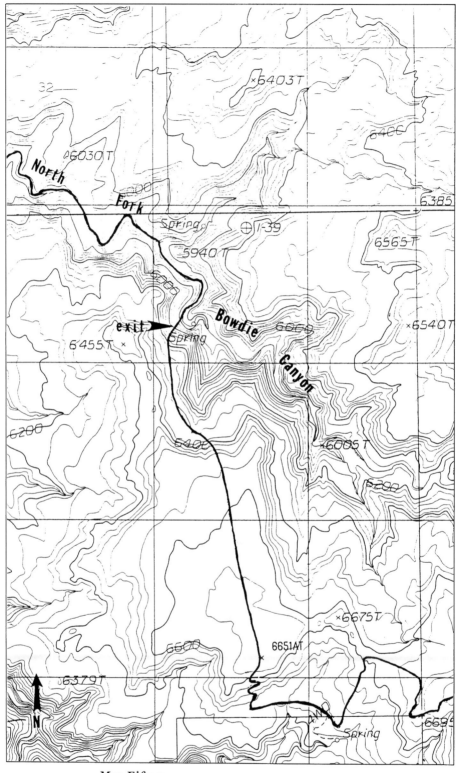

Map Fifteen

Arch in Bowdie Canyon.

more comfortable for cooking or perhaps camping. The canyon ends in a fall in another ten minutes (at elevation 6005T). The next reliable source of water is in Youngs Canyon. You will reach it at the end of Day Five. Load up with water here. (1.5–2.0 hours.)

Exit the North Fork

Exit the side canyon to the south on either side of its center. From the top go south. Stay on high ground. In twenty minutes you will intersect the edge of a canyon (near elevation 6651AT). You are in a no-man's-land between the North and South forks of Bowdie Canyon. No matter where you are on the rim, drop south down the cliffs to a wide red-floored pinyon and juniper terrace. Look for a little-used track that is difficult to locate. (Do not drop all the way to the bottom of the canyon.) The track improves as you follow it east. When the track starts to go up a thin layer of white sandstone, look for a "Tee." An indistinct track to the right (SW) goes to a medium spring at the base of a fall surrounded by cottonwoods. There is camping nearby. (The spring is shown on the map at the end of a 4WD track one-quarter mile northeast of elevation 6490T.) (2.0–2.5 hours.)

Water: This is a dry camp. Water has to be hauled from the

North Fork of Bowdie Canyon. Unless there have been recent rains, do not depend on the spring.

Option One—Alternate Day Five. 6.0 to 8.0 hours. Bowdie Canyon East and Black Steer Canyon maps. There is no reliable water along the route. There is water at the end of the day.

Into Youngs Canyon

(**Bowdie Canyon East map.**) Backtrack from the spring to the original track and follow it generally east out of the canyon. Ignore all side tracks. In one hour you will reach a burned, barren area at the top of a hill. This is Dark Canyon Plateau. The track leads to a stock pond (at elevation 7116T) which is full only after recent rains. Past the stock pond and before a corral, turn right (SW) off the main track onto a 4WD track. (Do not mistake this track for the track that joins the main track *before* the stock pond.)

In ten minutes the track divides; the track to the left leads to The Dugout, a unique and still-used line cabin. (**Map Sixteen.**) (The cabin site is shown on the Bowdie Canyon East map.) Follow the main track to the right. It goes south-southwest for a short distance across the sage-choked Horse Pasture, then ends. Cut west across Horse Pasture for a couple of hundred yards to a wash. Follow it down. Pass the first fall on a cattle trail to the left that takes you into the canyon. In a couple of minutes Youngs Canyon comes in from the left (E). There are medium potholes at the confluence. (2.5–3.5 hours.)

Down Youngs Canyon

Hike down the canyon. Pass the first small fall on the right. At the next fall (medium potholes), exit the canyon to the left (SE) up a steep hillside. (The exit is at the spring marked on the map; the spring is unreliable. There are medium potholes below the fall. The canyon ends shortly in a huge drop.)

Go southwest across a small drainage and struggle up Cedar Mesa cliffs to the top (many options). (**Black Steer Canyon map.**) Walk south on a juniper and pinyon plain for a half hour to the rim of a side canyon coming in from

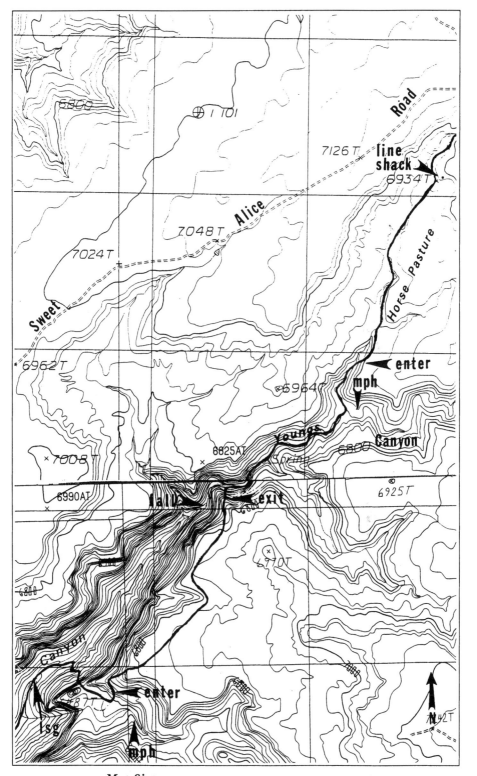

Map Sixteen

the southeast (shown one-half mile south of elevation 6970T). To get into the canyon, go to its southwest corner and find a cairned trail zigzagging southeast down the cliffs. There are medium potholes below a fall and there is camping in the area.

Look west down the side canyon. There is a black-and-white tower festooned with holes (elevation 6487T). Pass it on the right (N) side and follow a sparsely cairned trail down a long, steep slope into Youngs Canyon. There is a large spring at the base of the slope, but campsites are nonexistent.

In forty-five minutes the stream drops into a gorge with waterfalls and beckoning swim pools. There is camping in the area. (3.5–4.5 hours.)

> **Water:** There is always water in Youngs Canyon, though it occasionally does go underground for short distances.

Option One—Alternate Day Six. 5.5 to 7.0 hours. Black Steer Canyon and Indian Head Pass maps. There is water all along the route.

Down Youngs Canyon

(**Black Steer Canyon map.**) From the top of the gorge a trail skirts along the rim on the left (LDC)(S). Within five minutes note a high fall in the gorge. Past this, the trail drops fifty feet through a cliff-band to the right (N) to a bench. (If you travel too far along the rim a pinnacle below the rim of the canyon appears. Backtrack and find the trail.) Follow the bench down the canyon to a saddle between the pinnacle and the main cliff. Descend a steep slope south to the gray limestone floor of a side canyon. Follow it down to the main canyon.

The ensuing falls can be easily passed on trails to the left. The canyon ends in a medley of perfect falls and pools before joining Dark Canyon. Poison ivy can be a problem in the lower portion of Youngs Canyon. (1.5–2.0 hours.)

> **Digression:** Falls and pools continue up Dark Canyon for another hour or so. Above that the canyon is often dry. (2.0–3.0 hours round-trip.)

Down Dark Canyon

Hike down Dark Canyon. This stretch has an unbelievable number of small falls and delightful pools that run through layers of gray limestone (the upper member of the Hermosa Formation). Large groups will find few campsites, but small groups will have no problems. (**Indian Head Pass map.**) (4.0–5.0 hours to the mouth of Lost Canyon.)

> **Water:** There is always water along this stretch of Dark Canyon.

Option One—Alternate Day Seven. 3.0 to 4.0 hours. Indian Head Pass map. There is water in Dark Canyon.

To the trailhead

(**Indian Head Pass map.**) From Lost Canyon it takes twenty-five minutes to reach the bottom of the Sundance Trail. Follow it back to the trailhead. (3.0–4.0 hours.)

The Young Turks

I met Rob Roseen at the foot of the Sundance Trail in Dark Canyon one winter some years ago. Although the group he was with had gone downcanyon on a dayhike, Rob had remained behind with a cold and a sore throat. Since I spend most of my time alone, I was happy to take Rob up on his offer of a hot drink. I was immediately impressed with Rob—his energy, his bright outlook, and his love of canyon country. We chatted for an hour or more and, as I rose to leave, Rob suggested that we do a desert adventure together. As usually happens in such situations, I put Rob's proposal on the back burner and didn't think of it for a year or more. However, I was pleasantly surprised when Rob dropped me an occasional note. Thus, when I was planning a "Sheer Terror" week, I invited Rob.

The "Sheer Terror" week is a yearly gathering of canyoneers and rock climbers from across the nation. Participants are intent on descending technical slots—canyons that are so narrow and challenging that few are able to make it through them. Rob showed up in Hanksville on the appointed day with his climbing partner Rob May. The two Robs were to turn our heads and change our views about the potential of hardcore canyoneering.

Both Robs were nineteen at the time and were in school: Rob Roseen in Massachusetts studying environmental technology and Rob May in Washington State working toward a degree in physics. They provided a sharp contrast to the others in our group. Most of us were approaching forty and were a bit staid in our ways. The Robs, with their youthful vigor hearkened back to the sixties; each wore his long blond hair in a ponytail and was adorned with assorted jewelry.

Rob May belaying Rob Roseen in Long Canyon.

For a week we worked the slots, making some, failing on others. It quickly became apparent that the Robs were preternaturally skilled. We soon found it was easiest to let them lead the most difficult pitches. Like competent inventors, they devised new techniques as the terrain dictated. Wall-running was developed as a means of crossing unfathomably deep potholes that were too wide to simply jump and, with smooth vertical walls on either side, too sheer to climb around. The Robs would stand back and, with a burst of speed, would somehow run across the vertical walls to the far side of the pothole. We had been doing similar maneuvers for years but had never taken it to the same extremes as the Robs. At times they would cover forty feet or more, seeming to defy the laws of gravity in the process. Anchorless rappels, train belays, and leaps of faith were among the products of their skill and vision. We started calling them the Young Turks.

I had explored both Long and Gravel canyons and had been able to ascend the former but not descend the latter. I had had to bypass what appeared to be a stupendous stretch of impossible narrows. But the Young Turks, Harvey Halpern, and I were able to spend a week in Gravel Canyon exploring every nook and cranny. We were constantly amazed at the variety of the challenges and the beauty of the area.

The "impossible" narrows turned out to be some of the most problem-filled in canyon country. Although the use of bolts would have substantially reduced the difficulty, it is against the canyoneering ethic to mar the rocks. We left it up to the Robs to devise new techniques and lead the hardest sections. This they did with alacrity. At times we found ourselves chimneying far above the floor of the canyon; at other times, we were squeezing through the tiniest of slots or rappeling down cliffs into darkness so profound we couldn't see the bottom. Several of the rappels ended in deep pools of bitterly cold water, which made it difficult for us to unclip from the ropes and keep our packs and cameras dry. After making it through the crux narrows, we found we were out of time, and we therefore had to skip the lower portion of the canyon. A year later, Ginger Harmon, Larry Breed, and Jim Finch joined me for an integral descent of Gravel Canyon.

White Canyon

I clawed, contorted, chimneyed, groveled, grabbed, giggled, got belayed, pressed, paddled, prayed, raced, rappeled, raved, swam, squeezed, slithered, slipped, slid, shimmied, straddled, stemmed, sometimes actually walked, saw the reliquiae of the ancient ones, and emerged from the mouth of the canyon worn-out, ragged, and happy.

Ginger Harmon on Gravel Canyon, 1992

General description: It seems that canyon hikes fit into one of two categories. The longer routes tend to go from one amazing locale to the next, with perhaps some long stretches of inconsequential scenery in between. The shorter routes are often intense in their beauty, but they end long before one has a chance to settle into the rhythm so necessary for complete enjoyment. The Long Canyon–Gravel Canyon loop solves both problems; it provides a never-ending series of incredible narrows, a plethora of prehistoric sites, and enough physical and technical challenges to reinvigorate even the most jaded canyoneer.

The White Canyon area was populated by the Anasazi Indians from the late Basketmaker through the Pueblo III periods (A.D. 500 to A.D. 1300). The best examples of the cliff dwellings they left behind can be seen along the upper reaches of White Canyon in Natural Bridges National Monument. Smaller dwellings, petroglyph and pictograph panels, and lithic scatters can be found in most of the White Canyon tributaries.

Settlers moved into the White Canyon area in the 1860s and used it for grazing their cattle. The vertical walls of White Canyon prompted historian Neal Lambert to write about the futility of running cattle in the canyon. He claimed that "the beauty of these cliffs and canyons might well have been lost to the frustrated cowboys who tried to traverse them. Often a rider would have to detour for miles before he could find a break in the sheer walls of the wash [White Canyon]. Thus a cow just a few hundred yards away on the other side of White Canyon wash might just as well be in the next state. The ride was just about as long to one place as to the other."

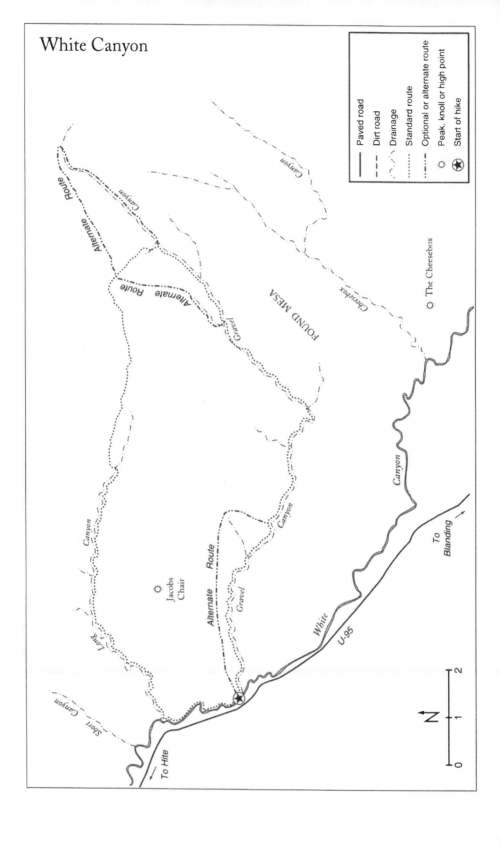

White Canyon

Legend:
- Paved road
- Dirt road
- Drainage
- Standard route
- Optional or alternate route
- Peak, knoll or high point
- Start of hike

The Cheesebox

FOUND MESA

Alternate Route

Canyon

Cheesebox

Gravel

Canyon

Alternate Route

Alternate Route

Gravel

Canyon

Jacobs Chair

White Canyon

U-95

To Blanding

Long Canyon

Short Canyon

To Hite

N

0 1 2

Zane Grey was captivated by the rugged nature of White Canyon and used it as a backdrop in several of his books. His stories about outlaws, shoot-outs, and Indian raids echo the real life escapades that took place in the canyon.

The roads on the plateaus between canyons are the remnants of the uranium boom. Though there was lots of activity, little uranium was found in the area.

The route starts at the Gravel Crossing of White Canyon. After a short jaunt down White Canyon, the route wanders up Long Canyon with its demanding narrows cut into Cedar Mesa Sandstone. A cross-country hop leads into peerless Gravel Canyon. Days can be spent there exploring side canyons, working through endless constrictions, and finding routes over, under, and around an interminable profusion of problems.

Trip length:	Four days minimum. Layover days and digressions can add two or three more days. Six days are recommended.
Elevation range:	4720′ to 7000′.
Recommended seasons:	March 15 to June 1 and September 1 to November 1. There is a lot of wading and swimming on this trip, so air temperatures should be reasonably warm. There is a flash-flood potential in both canyons.
Maps:	7.5-series USGS topographic maps: Black Steer Canyon, Indian Head Pass, Jacobs Chair, Mancos Mesa NE, and The Cheesebox. Metric map: Hite Crossing.
Skill level:	This is a technical route that should be attempted only by experienced canyoneers and competent rock climbers. There are many short climbing pitches up to Class 5.4 in difficulty. There are two rappels. They can be bypassed, but only at the expense of missing some of the best parts of Gravel Canyon. The leader must be familiar with belay techniques and be capable of leading the climbing sections without protection. There are several places with lots

of exposure. There may be long stretches of wading and swimming that cannot be avoided.

Special equipment: Wading shoes are essential. An old pair of hiking shoes is recommended; tennis shoes do not supply sufficient support. At least one inner tube per group should be carried for floating packs. Large plastic bags are helpful for keeping gear dry. One 165-foot climbing rope, a couple of lengths of sling material, and four rappel rings are required. A sit-harness and rappel device (Tuber, Figure-8, etc.) should be carried by every participant. Each hiker should have a minimum water capacity of six quarts. Even when the weather is hot, the narrows can be chilly. Be prepared.

Notes: This is one of the least-visited areas covered in the guide. There are no established campsites or fire rings. Please keep it that way.

Administering agency: San Juan Resource Area, Bureau of Land Management, 435 N. Main, Monticello, Utah 84535. (801-587-2141) In case of an emergency, there is a park ranger and a telephone at Hite Marina.

Land status: In 1979 the BLM dropped all of the lands covered in this chapter from its wilderness inventory, declaring that the areas dropped "clearly and obviously lack wilderness character." All of the lands covered in this hike are included in the Utah Wilderness Coalition proposal for wilderness designation—a proposal that seems to have a better understanding both of what wilderness is and its value.

ROAD SECTION

The unsigned track to the Gravel Crossing trailhead starts at mile 64.8 on Highway 95, the road that runs between the town of Blanding and Hite Marina. The track is suitable for light-duty vehicles, but it may be impassable when wet. There is camping at the parking circle. Driving time from Hite Marina is one-half hour.

0.0 | —Mileage starts at Highway 95 and goes northeast.

0.2 | —Parking circle on the rim of White Canyon. There is no trail register. You can continue driving down the track into White Canyon; but if you cross it you may not get back if it rains while you are hiking. (Gravel Crossing is labeled on the **Jacobs Chair map**.)

Geology lesson: The walls of White Canyon are Cedar Mesa Sandstone. Look across the canyon. The brown cliffs are Organ Rock Shale topped with a thin layer of White Rim Sandstone. Above the White Rim are the thin brown layers of the Moenkopi Formation and above them are the gray slopes of the Chinle Formation. Jacobs Chair, the impressive tower to the northeast, is carved from Wingate Sandstone.

Historical note: Although White Canyon had been used since the 1860s by ranchers and outlaws, the area is indelibly linked with Al Scorup, who arrived with a small herd of cattle in 1891. Often called the "Mormon Cowboy," Al, and his brother Jim, slowly built up a herd until it numbered in the thousands. Over a sixty-year period, Al's Scorup-Somerville Cattle Company dominated the rangelands near White Canyon, on Elk Ridge (which he called the Bear's Ears Plateau), and in Dark Canyon. Al named the Woodenshoe Buttes to the north of White Canyon; he claimed they reminded him of the wooden clogs his grandmother had worn.

Jacobs Chair was named for one of Al Scorup's cowboys, Frank Jacob Adams, who died while trying to cross White Canyon during a flash flood. He told his companions, "Ah, hell, you c'n cross this." His body was found a day later, four miles downcanyon.

Days One and Two. 6.5 to 13.0 hours without digressions. Jacobs Chair, Mancos Mesa NE, and Indian Head Pass maps. There are large potholes throughout White and Long canyons.

Warning: Youth groups often seek out canyons where

physical and technical challenges can be used to test their mettle. This is **not** the route for them. The technical aspects of this route are well beyond those who are not exceptionally experienced.

Note: The most surprising thing about hiking in Long and Gravel canyons is how variable conditions can be. On one trip a pothole may be deep and difficult to negotiate; the next time it may be full of sand and easy to wade. The time you spend in the canyons depends on current conditions and on the time you spend exploring side canyons. The only parameter that is important is that you must get from the top of Long Canyon to Gravel Canyon in one day. For this reason, plan on camping near the exit route out of Long Canyon, whether it takes one or two days to get there. I prefer the more reasonable pace of two days. The times allotted are the averages of many trips through the canyons and, as you will notice, they vary considerably. There are large potholes and good camping in both Long and Gravel canyons. Even a short rain will cause these canyons to flash flood; therefore camp well above the canyon floor.

Down White Canyon
(**Jacobs Chair map** and **Map Seventeen.**) Hike north down White Canyon. Long Canyon enters from the right (E) in about an hour. The mouth of the canyon is narrow and often muddy. There are large potholes and excellent camping in the area. (1.0–1.5 hours.)

Digression: Without packs, continue down White Canyon for one-half hour to the first canyon coming in on the right (S). (**Mancos Mesa NE map.**) This is Short Canyon. It has a good petroglyph panel on a south-facing wall and a granary near its mouth. The canyon ends in a short stretch of narrows. (1.0–2.0 hours round-trip.)

Up Long Canyon
Ten minutes up Long Canyon you pass a fall on a constructed cattle trail to the left (LUC). Keep your eyes open for several petroglyph and pictograph panels as you make your way upcanyon.

In about one and a half hours you reach the first set of narrows. There will be some wading and possibly a short swim. Rock climbers can avoid many of the potholes by

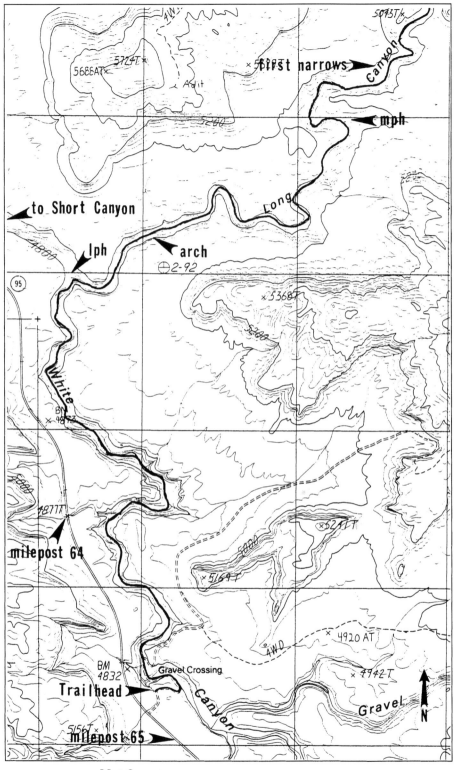

Map Seventeen

White Canyon near the mouth of Long Canyon.

stemming across or climbing around them. (2.0–4.0 hours, depending on how much trouble you have in the narrows.)

The canyon opens a tad and divides. Stay with the main canyon to the right (NNE) (south of elevation 5043T). Intermittent wading and mud-slogging continue. The canyon opens from time to time. There are several campsites. Large potholes appear now and again.

Jim Finch, Larry Breed, and Ginger Harmon hiking slickrock in Long Canyon.

The canyon widens and divides at a prow. Stay in the main canyon to the right (E). (The canyon to the left is shown one-half mile west of "Long" on the **Indian Head Pass map**.) (1.0–2.0 hours.)

> **Digression:** The canyon to the left (N) is worth a short walk. (0.5 hours round-trip.)

The crux narrows

The canyon narrows and the fun begins. There are two ways to deal with the quarter-mile-long crux narrows. The easiest and sanest method is to wade or swim the pools. There is a slippery climb out at the end. Rock climbers can stem most of the obstacles or, in one case, they can chimney up to a thin ledge on the right (LUC) (Class 5.8, 15′) and traverse over the worst part. The narrows end at a side canyon coming in from the left (N) (shown to the west of elevation 5337AT). (1.5–3.0 hours, depending on how long the crux narrows take.)

> **Digression:** The side canyon is worth a quick trip. (0.5 hours round-trip.)

To the exit canyon

Upcanyon there is more wading, several short climbing challenges (up to Class 5.4, 12′), and route-finding difficulties. After a long, lush section the canyon opens and divides in an area of fluted slickrock flooring. The main canyon goes around a U-shaped corner to the right (LUC)(S), narrows, and then ends at a fall. The short canyon to the left (LUC)(NE) is the exit canyon. There is camping at the confluence. (Long Canyon goes off of the **Indian Head Pass map** and onto the **Jacobs Chair map** for a short stretch before returning to the **Indian Head Pass map**. The exit canyon is shown immediately above the "74" on the edge of the **Indian Head Pass map**.) (1.0–2.5 hours.)

Water: There are large potholes below the confluence and medium springs in the dead-end main fork.

Note: If there is time, you may want to jump-start Day Three since it is a long one.

Day Three. 8.0 to 11.0 hard hours. Indian Head Pass, Jacobs Chair, The Cheesebox, and Black Steer Canyon maps. There is no reliable water until the end of the day.

Out of Long Canyon
    (**Indian Head Pass map.**) From the mouth of the exit canyon, scramble up a steep, boulder-filled gully to the left (LUC)(NW) for 100 feet to the first ledge. From the ledge look across the main canyon to the east-south-east. Find a break in the upper cliffs. Make your way to the break and ascend it.
    You are now out of the inner gorge of Long Canyon. Follow the rim of the canyon generally east across slickrock and on a juniper-and-pinyon plain. The walking is easy and there are many small potholes and fine slickrock camping.
    At the head of the canyon, you will find yourself surrounded by brown Organ Rock Shale walls. (You have gone from the **Indian Head Pass map** to the **Jacobs Chair map** and are now on **The Cheesebox map**.) From the very end of the canyon (at elevation 5875T) go east, to the left (N) side of a prow. (**Map Eighteen.**) The exit

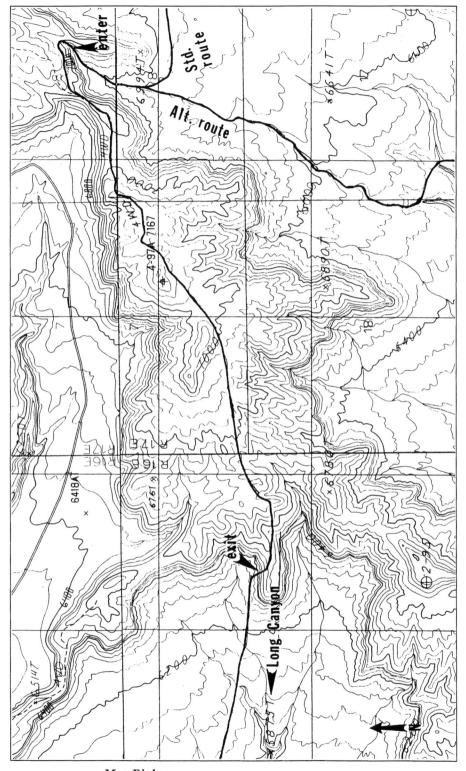

Map Eighteen

is not obvious but it is the only possible route out of the canyon at this point. Scramble up a steep slope, then climb a short wall (Class 5.1, 10′) through a thin layer of White Rim Sandstone. This is followed by an easier ramp (Class 4+, 10′) and another steep scramble to the top. (2.5–3.5 hours.)

Without packs, go west to the end of the prow. The views are great.

> *West-southwest:* The Wingate-walled Jacobs Chair.
> *West:* The two peaks in the distance are the Little Rockies: Mt. Holmes (7,998′) is the closest; Mt. Ellsworth (8,235′) is the farthest away.
> *Northwest:* The three tallest peaks of the Henry Mountains are, from nearest to farthest: Mt. Ellen (11,506′), Mt. Pennell (11,132′), and Mt. Hillers (10,737′).

To Gravel Canyon

Go east-northeast across a drainage and up a hill. Intersect an unused mining track. Follow the track to the left (N) for twenty minutes until the road goes over a pass. (The track is shown as a 4WD road on **The Cheesebox** and **Black Steer Canyon maps.**)

Again, the views are terrific.

> To the *North:* The Block is in the distance. To the right of it is the Big Ridge near the Maze District of Canyonlands National Park. The canyon directly below is Lost Canyon, which drains into Dark Canyon. The track goes from Highway 95 to South Elk Ridge above Natural Bridges National Monument.

Seven minutes from the pass the track divides. Stay to the right (SE). The track goes to the bottom of a hill, up a small rise, and drops to a narrow bridge between two canyons. You will leave the track here. (The narrow area is shown one-half mile west of elevation 6825AT.) (1.0–1.5 hours.)

From the lowest part of the narrow bridge look east into the head of a canyon. A precipitous chute drops west into the canyon. Descend the chute (Class 3+) and walk down the canyon for a couple of minutes until it is possible to cut east-southeast across a pinyon-and-juniper plain to the first drainage going south (shown one-quarter mile east of elevation 6994T on **The Cheesebox map.**) Follow the drainage south, down to the head of a small side canyon that goes into Gravel Canyon. Walk along the right-hand rim (LDC)(S) until you find a route down the Cedar Mesa cliff to the floor of the canyon. There are several possibilities, but it will take some scouting to find an easy route. (If you go too far up or down the canyon it will be very difficult to find a route down the Cedar Mesa walls.) (1.5–2.0 hours.)

> **Alternate route:** There are two other routes into Gravel Canyon. The first is a faster route that should be used only if water or time are in short supply, since if you take it you will miss the best narrows on the trip. Instead of cutting east-southeast to the next drainage, simply continue down the drainage to the south (shown one-eighth mile west of elevation 6994T). At a drop, where the canyon deepens, go left (E) for several minutes and cross another drainage. Follow the rim of the canyon south for several more minutes. Find a steep route into the canyon. Follow the canyon down until you are above Gravel Canyon. See "Water" section below for water sources. (2.5–3.0 hours.)
>
> The second route enters the top of Gravel Canyon and should be used only if water is not a problem. Instead of going down one of the drainages, cut northeast across the pinyon-and-juniper plain. Stay parallel to the Organ Rock Shale walls that are to the left (NW). **(Black Steer Canyon map.)** You will intersect Gravel Canyon at its head. (Do not try to drop into the canyon too soon or you won't be able to find a route down the Cedar Mesa cliff.) The canyon has innumerable obstacles and narrows to find a route around, and it contains a small natural bridge to climb over. It also contains many medium potholes. **(The Cheesebox map.)** (3.0– 4.5 hours to the confluence mentioned below.)

Down Gravel Canyon

Go down Gravel Canyon. Below the confluence of four forks of the canyon (above "Gravel" on the map), it narrows and becomes especially attractive. Pass a high drop into a narrows on a ledge to the right (LDC). You can either drop back into the canyon as soon as possible and enjoy the medium potholes dotting the gorge and the interesting route-finding and boulder-hopping problems, or you can stay on the ledge until a major side canyon (shown to the west of elevation 6580T) comes in on the left (LDC)(W) and drop back into the canyon near its mouth (Class 3+). (1.5–2.0 hours.)

Again the canyon narrows and the hiking becomes harder. Long stretches of route-finding around huge boulders are interspersed with astounding narrows. The next major side canyon (shown to the east of elevation 6281T) comes in on the right (N). It does not join the main canyon at floor level but rather at a pour-off below a narrow slot. (If you go too far downcanyon you will find yourself in a remarkable bowl that precedes a formidable stretch of narrows. The only way to the bottom of the bowl is to rappel, and there is no easy way through the narrows. Backtrack for a quarter mile to the side canyon/slot, which is now on your left (LUC)(N).) Note a steep ramp going up to the slot (Class 4+). It leads to a large pothole.

From the slot, hike up the main canyon for 200 yards and exit via a broken ramp on the left (LUC)(N)(Class 3+). Make your way over slickrock into the side canyon above the slot. There is excellent slickrock camping in the area. (1.5–2.0 hours.)

Water: There are medium potholes at the head of the slot. If they are not full, haul water from the previously mentioned large pothole at the base of the slot.

Digression: The side canyon is great to explore and is full of worthwhile surprises. (2.0–3.0 hours round-trip.)

Rock-climber's note #1: There is an interesting route out of Gravel Canyon on its left (LDC)(S) side. From the base of the exit ramp go upcanyon for 100 yards and ascend a steep slope behind several huge boulders on the right (LUC)(S). At the top of the slope and behind a thin, tall oak tree, climb up a vertical wall by using a row of Moqui steps (Class 5.3, 25'). You can continue downcanyon along ledges and drop to the canyon floor after forty-five minutes.

Rock-climber's note #2: The formidable stretch of narrows that was circumvented in the standard route has been descended. This may be one of the most awesome and demanding slots in all of canyon country. Be prepared for a half-dozen or more rappels, several swims, long stretches of difficult chimneying and stemming, and an assortment of miscellaneous perils. This slot should only be attempted by experienced canyoneers who are accomplished rock climbers and who are familiar with sophisticated canyoneering techniques. **This is not the place for inexperienced hikers or novice rock climbers.**

Days Four through Six. 8.0 to 14.5 hours without digressions. The Cheesebox and Jacobs Chair maps. There are large potholes scattered throughout this stretch.

Note: The route descriptions of days four through six have been combined. Water and campsites can be found on a regular basis. Every side canyon contains a treasure of one sort or another, whether it is a hanging garden, a set of narrows, or relics of previous habitation. Although the route takes you around many narrows that cannot be conveniently entered from the top, they are all worth inspecting from the bottom. With so much to explore, three days may not be enough time, though a hardy group could hike out in one day.

Down Gravel Canyon
From the side canyon follow Cedar Mesa benches downcanyon.

Digression: The first side canyon coming in on the right (shown to the east of elevation 6108AT) is interesting and ends in a fine set of narrows. Pass the first fall on the right (LUC). (1.0 hour round-trip.)

There are no serious obstacles, but a pack lift may be needed in one spot. Below the mouth of the narrows, find a route down to the floor of the canyon. (1.0–1.5 hours.)

The canyon immediately plunges into another stretch of narrows. Pass it on either side. Also pass the next narrows on either side. The next major landmark is a canyon coming in from the left (E) (shown to the southeast of elevation 5645T on the Jacobs Chair map.) (1.0–1.5 hours.)

Digression: This long side canyon has great narrows. There may be some wading across potholes. Rock climbers may be

Tunnel in Gravel Canyon. Photo by Harvey Halpern.

able to stem and chimney across them. There are exit routes near the head of the canyon. (The mouth of the canyon starts on the Jacobs Chair map, but the canyon ends on The Cheesebox map.) (1.5–2.0 hours round-trip.)

Pass the next fall on the right (LDC). Look for a natural bridge in the gorge below. A short distance downcanyon is another set of narrows. If they are dry, walk down the canyon. If wet, they can be skirted on the right (LDC). (1.0–1.5 hours.)

Digression: If you do go around the narrows on the right, the side canyon coming in from the right (N) (east of 2-105 on the map) has large potholes near its mouth. This side canyon is a joy to explore. Pass a fall on either side. The canyon ends in impressive narrows. (1.0–1.5 hours round-trip.)

The first rappel

Continue down the canyon. The first rappel comes in one hour. (The rappel site is north of elevation 5410T.) There are large potholes in the short narrows before the drop and good camping on slickrock sheets. (1.0–1.5 hours.)

The rappel itself should be done from one of the half-dozen trees on the left (LDC) side of the canyon. The rappel is about seventy feet in length, but check this yourself.

Jacobs Chair from Gravel Canyon.

Alternate route: If you are not equipped to rappel, you can leave the canyon here and hike directly to White Canyon. Exit the canyon via a steep slab to the right (LDC) (Class 4, 35′) that is just upcanyon from a couple of caves high on a wall. From the top, go north, head Cowboy Canyon, and proceed generally west between Gravel Canyon and an escarpment to the north. You will intersect a rarely used track that goes to Gravel Crossing. There is no water along the route. (4.0–5.0 hours.)

Below the rappel the walking is easy, and in forty-five minutes Cowboy Canyon comes in on the right (NE) (1.0–2.0 hours.)

Digression: Cowboy Canyon has huge cottonwoods at its mouth and is rewarding to explore. (0.5 hours round-trip.)

The second rappel
A few minutes down from Cowboy Canyon you pass a fall on the right (LDC) on a wide ledge. The ledge narrows. Cross a boulder field and continue along the rim of the canyon.

Digression: There is an escape route out of the canyon to the right (LDC), immediately past the boulder field.

Jim Finch on the second rappel in Gravel Canyon.

You will have to rappel back into the canyon. With careful searching, you can find a place where the rappel is only thirty feet long. Trees can be used to anchor your rope. (1.0–1.5 hours.)

Wading and swimming

There are no more rappels, but the canyon does not become any less interesting. The walking is easy, with only

Larry Breed swimming the narrows of Gravel Canyon.

occasional small problems, until near the end of the canyon. It then narrows (southwest of elevation 4942T) and there may be a couple of long stretches of deep wading or swimming. There are several escape routes before the narrows. A short stroll takes you to White Canyon.

Hike down White Canyon to Gravel Crossing. (2.0–5.0 hours depending on how much you have to swim.)

Winter

What to do? what to do? It was mid-February and Escalante country was buried under a foot of snow. The Hole-in-the Rock road and the Burr Trail were impassable and I wanted to go backpacking! The problem was not in the hiking—the snow is just a nuisance—but in driving to a trailhead. After looking over the maps, I decided to try to find a route to Boulder Creek from Highway 12. The route was successful and I spent an enjoyable ten days exploring Boulder and Deer creeks, The Gulch, Horse Canyon, and the benchlands in between.

Twenty years later, and I am again faced with the same dilemma: it is winter and I want to hike in Escalante country. Now, though, the Burr Trail has been paved and, even though snow-covered, it is passable in my two-wheel-drive van. I motor to The Gulch trailhead in a snowstorm. My goal is to put together a loop hike that requires no wading in the Escalante River.

Over the years, I have come to realize that as wonderful as Escalante country is, the worst part is the river itself. Constantly wading over slippery boulders, groveling up steep riverbanks, fighting off the seasonal influx of biting flies, and clawing through interminably long stretches of willow, tamarisk, and sage are not my idea of a good time. Many may disagree, but I wince when I think of the great numbers of young men and women I run into on the river. It is a rare group that seems to be having fun. More often than not, their feet look like raw hamburger and their clothes are ripped and torn. After a few hard days on the river they no longer marvel at the splendor of the vertical walls or take the time to explore the side canyons. Their heads are down and they are content to make it to camp by evening. My brother's wife, Donna, is typical. She hiked the length of the Escalante from Calf Creek to

Forty Mile with a university group many years ago. It was her last backpack trip; the physical discomfort outweighed the grandeur of the area and ruined her love of long hikes.

With snow on the ground, I was doubly determined to avoid wading in the river. On previous trips I had pinpointed what I considered to be the prettiest areas on the east side of the Escalante. On this trip I wanted to tie all the pieces together into a viable route. Deer Creek seemed the logical starting point, but most of its length is choked with brush and the creek can be deep and cold. However, the area near the confluence of Boulder and Deer creeks is one of the highlights of the Escalante. Likewise, The Gulch is stupendous in its lower reaches; but the upper portion is less scenic and is often trashed by cattle. By starting at The Gulch trailhead and going overland to the confluence of Boulder and Deer creeks, I avoided one problem—wading down Deer Creek. A route over Brigham Tea Bench into the lower reaches of The Gulch solved another; I was able to avoid the upper part of The Gulch. The route out of The Gulch proved to be a challenge: snow on the rock made the climb treacherous. But the benchlands leading into Horse Canyon were windswept and dry.

The hiker who sticks to the canyon floors is missing a large part of what canyon country has to offer. It is the barren slickrock and the rolling sage-covered hills on the benches between canyons that provide the best views and often the best camping. In winter, when the canyons are cold and dark, the uplands are bathed in sunlight and warm alcoves can be sought out for rest breaks or lunch. I have rarely camped in a canyon during the winter. The short days and long cold nights are enough to test anyone's resolve without having to wait the extra hours for the sun to find the canyon floor.

Horse Canyon at its junction with Wolverine Creek and Little Death Hollow is akin to a major highway interchange—constructed cattle trails and canyons branch off every which way. On this trip I followed a cattle trail out of Horse Canyon, traversed Big Bown Bench, and dropped into Silver Falls Creek near its confluence with the Escalante by climbing down a steep wall. Silver Falls Creek could be thought a misnomer: it doesn't contain silver, a fall, or a creek. It was named for its stunning, varnish-streaked walls that shine like silver when wet.

Silver Falls Creek, which is firm-floored and dry in its upper reaches, led to the top of Little Death Hollow. On previous trips I had used Wolverine Creek to arrive at the same point; but, although the Silver Falls Creek route is a day or so longer, I enjoyed it more. Little Death Hollow, with its seductive side slots, an arch, and a long stretch of provocative narrows, was the finest part of the trip. Back at the interchange in Horse Canyon, I found a still-used cattle trail and followed it back into The Gulch and to the trailhead.

The Escalante East

Some of us do not move very rapidly along the main channel. It is not that our packs are heavy, that we are lazy, that we cannot find our footing, that we cannot decide whether to take the meanders midstream or to shave the corners through the weeds. It is that every few bends there is a breach in the walls, luring us into a darker world which must also be explored.

Bruce Berger, 1990

General description: The Escalante River starts high on the Aquarius Plateau and ends one hundred twenty-five miles later in the still waters of Lake Powell. In the intervening miles, the river has cut a deep and complex gorge replete with long side canyons, bucolic pasturelands, exciting slots, and a host of pinnacles, ponderosa-lined potholes, and prodigious arches and natural bridges. After many trips to the area, desert explorer Kent Frost was prompted to write: "There is a fairy-tale quality to that canyon. Escalante is sliced from beautiful rock that has been sculptured on a grand scale. Every side canyon conceals an arch or cave or vault in sandstone colors of cream, beige, salmon, pink, and brown. The bottom is gentle and generous, with green plants, willows, and cottonwood trees beside the river."

The Escalante area has become known as one of the largest and most varied desert regions in the southwest. The eastern section of the Escalante River basin has an abundance of renowned canyons, some ten miles or more in length, that start high on the Waterpocket Fold, cut through the Circle Cliffs, and end at the river. Each of the canyons has an intensity of its own—an energy drawn from vibrant, green-fringed alcoves, shimmering tapestry walls, and gently flowing waters.

The Escalante area was first occupied by Indians of the Desert Archaic Culture (6500 B.C to 1500 B.C.). Little evidence of their habitation has been found. Most of the cliff structures and rock art you will see in the area covered by this chapter are Anasazi sites that date back to the Pueblo II and Pueblo III periods (A.D. 900 to A.D. 1300).

Settlers sent on a "mission" by Brigham Young, head of the Mormon Church, arrived in the Escalante Valley in

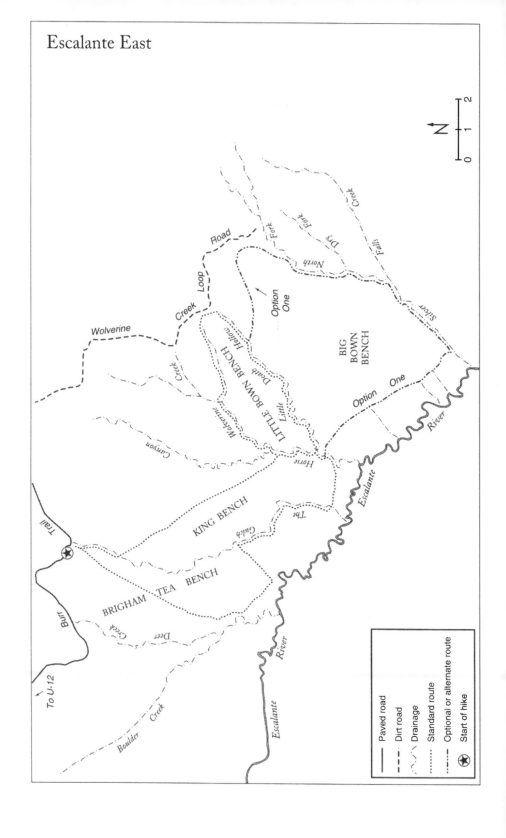

Escalante East

1876. The handiwork of the early pioneers is evident throughout the region. The Burr Trail was built by John Atlantic Burr in the late 1800s to move cattle from the Aquarius Plateau to Bullfrog Basin on the Colorado River. Burr died alone on the desert while trying to remedy a urinary tract blockage with a piece of wire.

Charles Hall, a member of the Hole-in-the-Rock expedition of 1879, built a road that went down Harris Wash, crossed the Escalante River, and continued up Silver Falls Creek. Portions of the old road are still visible. Uranium-mining roads were built into the Circle Cliffs area, but little serious mining was done in the Escalante area.

The route starts on the Burr Trail at the head of The Gulch. An overland trek leads to Boulder Creek near its confluence with Deer Creek, then crosses Brigham Tea Bench and drops into the middle section of The Gulch. After passing through the narrows of The Gulch, a route over the top of King Bench takes you into Horse Canyon. From Horse Canyon, a loop hike goes up Wolverine Creek, cuts behind the Circle Cliffs, and follows Little Death Hollow back down to Horse Canyon. A cattle trail leads back over King Bench, into The Gulch, and to the trailhead.

An optional route goes from Horse Canyon, across Big Bown Bench, and into Silver Falls Creek, which you follow through the Circle Cliffs. You return to Horse Canyon by way of Little Death Hollow. Though there are digressions that describe routes to the Escalante, there is no hiking in or along the river.

Trip length:	Six days minimum. Layover days, digressions, and an option can add a day or two more.
Elevation range:	4920′ to 6200′.
Recommended seasons:	March 1 to June 1 and September 1 to December 1. There is a flash-flood potential in most of these canyons.
Maps:	7.5-series USGS topographic maps: King Bench, Pioneer

Mesa, Red Breaks, and Silver Falls Bench.
Metric map: Escalante.

Skill level: This is a moderately strenuous route with difficult route-finding. There are a couple of short climbing pitches of up to Class 4+ in difficulty. Novices will need to be belayed. The leader must be familiar with belay techniques and be capable of leading the climbing sections without protection. There are several places with lots of exposure. There are short stretches of wading in shallow water.

Special equipment: Wading shoes are optional; an old pair of tennis shoes will suffice. A fifty-foot rope is adequate. Each member of the party should have the capacity to carry at least six quarts of water.

Notes: All of the canyons described in this hike are heavily used. Carry out your toilet paper when in the canyon bottoms. Campfires are allowed, but do not use them.

Escalante Outfitters, located in a large log cabin in the middle of the town of Escalante, has all the maps for this route. They also carry backpacking equipment, freeze-dried food, and white gas. Showers and cabins are also available. The Outfitters is open year-round. Their hours are 8:00 A.M. to 8:00 P.M., Monday through Saturday, and 1:00 P.M. to 6:00 P.M. on Sunday.

Administering agency: Escalante Resource Area. Bureau of Land Management, P.O. Box 225, Escalante, Utah 84726. (801-826-4291) There is a combined BLM and Glen Canyon NRA ranger station on the west side of the town of Escalante. From November through April, the ranger station is open Monday through Friday, 8:00 A.M. to 5:00 P.M. From May through October it is open seven days a week at the above times.

Land status: Except for several small areas near established roads, and Silver Falls Creek which is in the Glen Canyon NRA, all of this route is in the North Escalante Canyons/The Gulch Instant Study Area. The Instant Study Area classification was given to areas that had been deemed worthy of wilderness designation by the BLM before FLPMA. All of the lands covered in this hike are included in the Utah Wilderness Coalition proposal for wilderness designation.

ROAD SECTION

The Gulch trailhead is located on the Burr Trail, a partially paved road that runs from the small town of Boulder to either Bull Frog Marina on Lake Powell to the south or to Capitol Reef National Park to the north. The road starts in Boulder, which is on Highway 12 between the towns of Escalante and Torrey, and initially goes east. A sign reads Boulder–Bull Frog Scenic Road.

Cross Deer Creek in 6.3 miles. There is a small campground with pit toilets and garbage cans. After another 3.7 miles there is a trailhead sign to the right, just before the road drops into Long Canyon. Turn off the pavement and go 0.2 miles to the trailhead. There is a trail register. You can camp at the trailhead, but the camping is better farther down Long Canyon. (The trailhead is located at a sharp bend in the road between a labeled cliff dwelling and a corral on the **King Bench map**.)

Historical note: The present site of the town of Escalante was discovered in 1866 by a Mormon cavalry unit while they were pursuing a band of Indians. They called the area Potato or Spuds Valley because of the many wild potatoes they found.

In June 1872 Frederick Dellenbaugh and Almon Thompson, members of the second Powell expedition down the Colorado River, led a reconnaissance trip from Kanab, Utah, to the mouth of the Dirty Devil River. They had left a boat cached there six months before when the expedition had halted for the winter. After working their way over what are now called the Escalante Mountains, the group dropped into Potato Valley.

At first they thought the stream running through the valley was the Dirty Devil River. Frederick Dellenbaugh wrote in his diary: "Prof. [Almon Thompson] and Dodds then climbed to where they could get a wide view. . . . [The] Prof. perceived at once that we were not on the river we thought we were on, for by this explanation he saw that the stream we were trying to descend flowed into the Colorado far to the south-west of the Unknown [Henry] Mountain, whereas he knew positively that the Dirty Devil came in on the north-east. Then the question was, 'What river is this?' for we had not noted a tributary of any size between the Dirty Devil and the San Juan. It was a new river whose identity had not been fathomed."

Almon Thompson then named the "new river" for the Franciscan friar Silvestre Vélez de Escalante. Escalante and Padre Francisco Atanasio Domínguez led a group of the first white men known to have traversed the canyons of southern Utah. They passed south of the Escalante River in 1776 while searching for a route from Santa Fe to Los Angeles.

> **Note:** Because water availability is not a problem on this hike, the route is not described using a day-to-day format. Use the times shown in parentheses ( ) to help plan your itinerary.

Exit The Gulch

(**King Bench map** and **Map Nineteen.**) From the trailhead, look east. A steep hillside leads up to a narrow tree-covered ledge that goes to the left (E). Ascend the hill and traverse around the corner on the ledge. The Gulch is below you to the south. Clamber west up a series of cliff-bands to the top of a rise (elevation 5935).

> **Geology lesson:** Look north. The road goes up Long Canyon. The three formations of the Glen Canyon Group are visible. The sheer walls in the bottom of the canyon are Wingate Sandstone. The red, ledge-forming cliffs above are the Kayenta Formation, and the highest slickrock knobs and walls to the northwest are Navajo Sandstone.

Look southwest. There is a shallow saddle with a sandy slope leading up to it. To the left (SSW) is a slickrock knob dotted with trees (elevation 6197). Hike to the top of the knob. (1.0–1.5 hours.)

The views from the top of the knob are wonderful:

North-northwest: Boulder Mountain.
Northwest and west: The Aquarius Plateau.

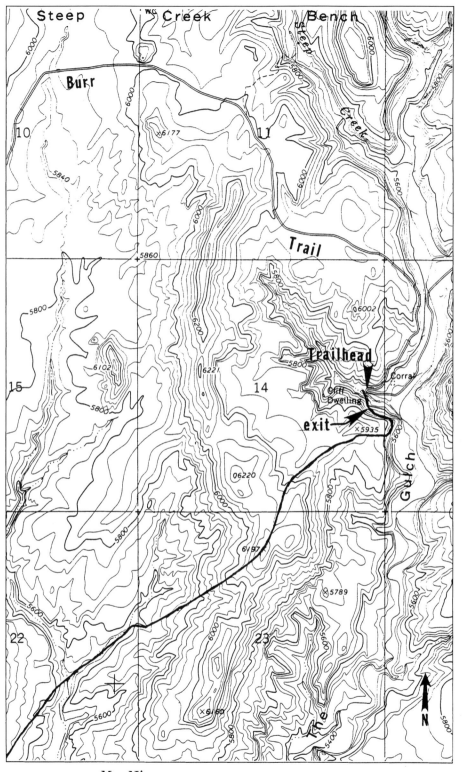

Map Nineteen

South: The long ridge in the distance is the Kaiparowits Plateau.

Southeast: The large round-topped peak is Navajo Mountain (10,346′).

East-northeast: The tops of the Henry Mountains are barely visible.

To Boulder Creek

Again look to the southwest. There is a long, white, Navajo escarpment running north to south on the far side of a valley. At the south end of the escarpment is a prominent, flat-topped, cone-shaped tower that is red on the bottom and white on top (elevation 6167). One mile to the right (N) is a smaller cone-shaped tower with a flat top (elevation 6209). Make your way across the valley to the south end of the southernmost dome (elevation 6167). There are many options. (1.5–2.5 hours.)

A mile to the south-southeast of the dome is a large slickrock monolith (elevation 5973). Hike across slickrock and pass the monolith on its left (E) side. You will cross an old log fence en route. Circle around the south end of the monolith and drop southwest into a slickrock-lined drainage. **(Map Twenty.)** (The map shows "Tanks" in this drainage. The "Tanks" are large potholes.) Follow the drainage down to a cliff overlooking Boulder Creek. The narrows of Boulder Creek are visible downcanyon. Search for a crease in a steep slab that can be used for getting in and out of the canyon (Class 4, 30′). There is fine camping on ledges along the creek or near the aforementioned "Tanks" on the slickrock. (2.0–3.5 hours.)

> **Alternate route:** This slightly longer alternative is for the slickrock aficionado. Hike across the valley into the gap to the right (N) of the northern cone-shaped tower (elevation 6209 on the map). Walk through the gap for a couple of hundred yards on gorgeous slickrock until the canyon floor starts to drop. You will exit the canyon here. (The canyon below (SW) is lined with huge potholes surrounded by cattails and ponderosa pines; it leads to the rim of Deer Creek, providing excellent views of the Deer Creek narrows.)
>
> Climb up a marvelously cross-stratified Navajo slab to the left (S). This looks difficult (Class 3+), but a little scouting will reveal a sensible route. If the route becomes too dif-

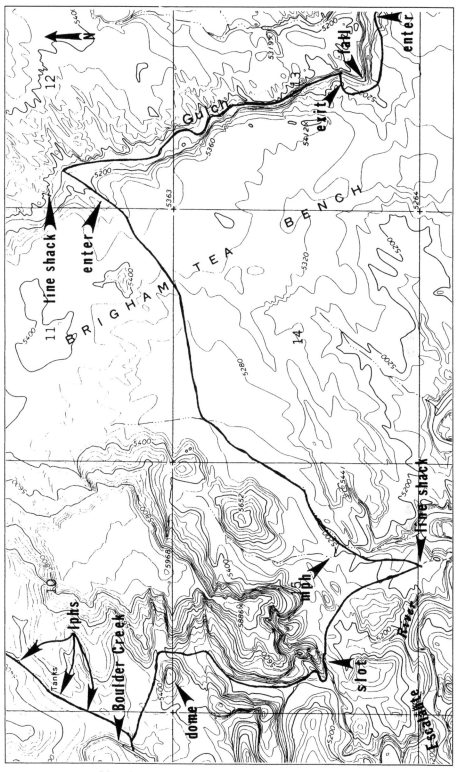

Map Twenty

The narrows of Boulder Creek.

ficult, you have not found the easiest line. At the top of the Navajo go between the cone to the left (N) (elevation 6209) and a smaller formation to the right (S). Descend steep slickrock south into a drainage and follow it downcanyon (SW). The drainage is lined with ponderosa pines and large potholes. There is good camping everywhere.

As you approach Deer Creek the gradient steepens into a succession of short falls and potholes. Do not try to go down the drops. Instead, exit the canyon to the left

(LDC)(S) and continue south into the next drainage. While walking along the rim between drainages you will see the junction of Deer and Boulder creeks. Below the confluence the combined canyon stream is called Boulder Creek. Walk down the drainage. Before it reaches Boulder Creek, the drainage passes the right (N) side of a checkerboard-faced dome; it then ends at a sheer drop. Before you pass the dome, cut southeast over a rise and drop into yet another drainage. This is the "Tanks" drainage. Follow this drainage down to a cliff overlooking Boulder Creek. (Add 1.5–2.5 hours.)

Digression: This is a wonderful place for a layover day; there is much to see and do. The narrows of Deer Creek are located in the mile above its confluence with Boulder Creek. There is a lot of wading. Boulder Creek above the confluence is easier to explore than is Deer Creek, though there also is some wading. Downcanyon, the narrows of Boulder Creek require swimming. From the bottom of the narrows you can return to the top by following the right-hand rim (LUC)(E) of the canyon. Brown and rainbow trout can be seen in the many deep pools found in both Boulder and Deer creeks.

To The Gulch

From the bottom of the "Tanks" drainage above Boulder Creek, look southeast. On the right is a large brown-gray dome; to the left is a red-and-white Navajo-walled escarpment. Hike through the gap between the dome and the escarpment and follow a canyon south until you are on a cliff above Boulder Creek. Make your way downcanyon along the rim for a quarter mile to a vertical wall. Descend a gully to Boulder Creek. Go down the creek for 150 yards and exit the canyon via a steep slot to the left (ENE). The slot (Class 4) becomes narrower and the rock looser near the top. Exit the top of the slot and work southeast, then south, to a handsome old line shack on a flat plain. (The shack and a short trail to the Escalante are shown on the map.)

There is a narrow canyon to the east of the line shack (shown one-quarter mile west of elevation 5441). Follow its left (LUC)(W) rim north until the narrows end; then follow the wash northeast. Stay to the right (E) of a

Line shack between Boulder Creek and The Gulch.

Navajo escarpment. After a half hour or so (time discrepancies won't matter) exit the wash, go due east across Brigham Tea Bench, and intersect the rim of The Gulch. There are many options for descending into the canyon. If the cliffs are vertical at the place you intersect the canyon, search upcanyon. The farther downcanyon one goes, the harder it is to find a satisfactory route. (Try to enter the canyon in the area represented between "The" and "Gulch" on the map.) There is a line shack immediately south of the "The." (2.5–3.5 hours.)

Down The Gulch

There is a perennial flow of water in The Gulch. As you walk downcanyon the walls close in and there may be short stretches of wading. At an abrupt left turn, the stream drops over a short fall into a narrow gorge (south-southeast of elevation 5412). It is wisest to explore these narrows from the bottom. To get around the narrows, first look downcanyon (E). Note a beautiful wall streaked with black and brown desert varnish that is framed by the narrows. Remember this wall.

Backtrack upcanyon for about four minutes to an indent in the cliff to the left (LUC)(W). There is a log against the cliff. Ascend a slab on downsloping holds to the right of the log (Class 4+, 20', belay beginners). This is the first possible exit out of the canyon. Continue up

Wading the narrows of The Gulch.

steep slabs to the top. Follow the rim downcanyon until you are even with the varnish-streaked wall. Look southeast. Below you is a vegetation-covered bench. A hiker-developed path will be visible. Go down a steep slab to the bench and follow the path into the canyon. (2.0–3.0 hours).

To the exit route

The canyon fluctuates between being moderately narrow and a tad wide. After one hour of hiking start looking for three potential exit canyons. (**Red Breaks map** and **Map Twenty-one.**) The three canyons are on the left (LDC)(E); they parallel each other and are only a minute or so apart. (The three canyons are shown between "The" and "King" on the map.)

The exit route

The first canyon comes in on the outside of a bend. It is to the left of an overhanging prow and its mouth is partially blocked by two cottonwoods—one alive and twisted, the other dead. This is the most difficult of the three canyons to negotiate.

The second canyon is one minute past the first and its mouth is partially blocked by a V-trunked cottonwood. This is the easiest canyon to exit if a pothole 100 yards upcanyon at the base of a short fall is not full. Scramble up

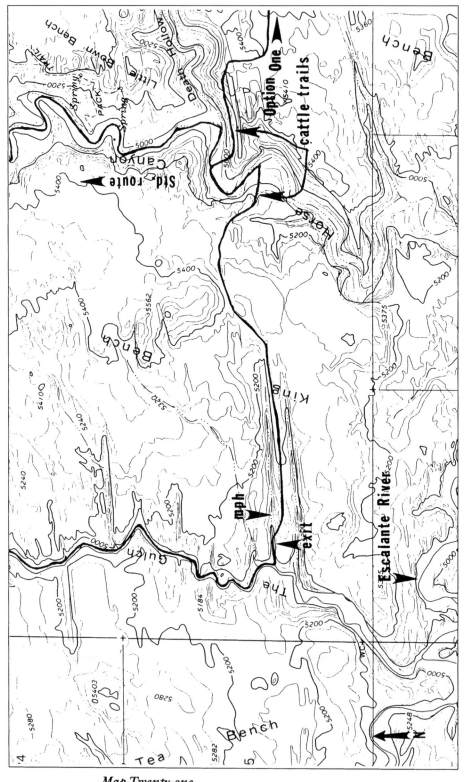

Map Twenty-one

the fall (Class 4, 30′) and immediately exit the canyon to the right (SE) by scrambling to the top up short walls and steep slabs. There is superb camping on undulating slickrock overlooking The Gulch.

The third canyon, yet another minute downcanyon, is my second choice. Start on a ledge on the left (LUC) side of the canyon. Above a fall, exit the canyon to the left as soon as possible. This puts you on the same undulating slickrock as does the previous exit. (2.0–3.0 hours.)

> **Digression:** To reach the Escalante, continue down The Gulch for a half hour. There are beaver ponds to cross and there may be knee-deep wading. The mouth of The Gulch is choked with tamarisk and sagebrush. There is poor camping along the river.

To Horse Canyon

Walk east up the slickrock. A prominent Navajo ridge with a U-shaped notch becomes visible to the east (elevation 5562). Continue east across King Bench and pass over the southern shoulder of the Navajo ridge. From the shoulder, you will be able to see the walls of Horse Canyon. The dark red, ledge-forming layer below the Navajo is the Kayenta Formation. To the northeast is the Kayenta-walled mouth of Little Death Hollow.

> **Historical note:** King Bench was named for John King, an early settler in the area.

> **Note:** The topographic map shows only a "Death Hollow." In an effort to differentiate this Death Hollow from the one near the top of Boulder Mountain, locals call this one Little Death Hollow.

Continue east, over the head of a drainage that runs south, to the edge of Horse Canyon. One bend downcanyon from the mouth of Little Death Hollow is a shallow east-facing indent in the otherwise vertical Navajo wall. The indent contains a steep slide and an old constructed cattle trail. Follow it to the canyon floor. There is a perennial flow of water and fair camping along this stretch of Horse Canyon. (1.0–1.5 hours.)

Digression: The hike down Horse Canyon to the Escalante takes about forty-five minutes. There is good camping along the river.

Option: See Option One for an alternate route that exits Horse Canyon and goes overland into Silver Falls Creek. The route then goes up the creek and returns to Horse Canyon via Little Death Hollow. This option adds one day to the hike and is worthwhile.

To Wolverine Creek

Hike up Horse Canyon, past the mouth of Little Death Hollow, to a line shack. The springs that feed the canyon start here. This is the last reliable water until halfway down Little Death Hollow, six to eight hours away. Load up with water here. Continue up Horse Canyon for twenty minutes to the mouth of Wolverine Creek, which comes in on the right (ENE). **(King Bench map.)**

Up Wolverine Creek

The first section of Wolverine Creek is wide, but the canyon quickly narrows as it enters the Wingate Sandstone. There may be several short stretches of shallow wading. After seventy-five minutes the canyon starts to widen, then divides. **(Pioneer Mesa map.)** Stay with the canyon to the right (E) (shown to the south of elevation 5883T). In another thirty minutes this canyon divides; again stay to the right (ENE). You are now walking in the Chinle Formation and may see segments of an old mining road. Twenty minutes further upcanyon the canyon divides once more; again stay to the right (E). In a half hour the canyon widens and ends as you pass through the Circle Cliffs. Simply stay parallel to the Wingate wall to the right as you circle around and start heading south into Little Death Hollow. You will pass across a corner of the Wolverine Petrified Wood Natural Area. You are not allowed to collect petrified wood here. (If you go too far out the top of the canyon, you will intersect a road. You can follow it southeast to a corral at the head of Little Death Hollow.) (4.0–5.0 hours.)

Down Little Death Hollow

The upper part of Little Death Hollow is wide, choked with Russian thistle, and not inspiring. Cattle trails, however, do make the hiking easy. In forty-five minutes a canyon comes in on the left (E). Past this, keep your eyes peeled for several petroglyph panels on large Wingate boulders to the right.

In an hour, after you pass an arch that is to the left (LDC) and then go through a short stretch of narrows, a narrow canyon comes in on the right (NW). Five minutes below it a more pronounced narrow canyon comes in on the right (NE) (shown to the east of elevation 5828T). Its mouth is partially blocked by trees. One hundred yards up this sand-floored canyon is a large pothole, which is the first reliable water since you left Horse Canyon. There is no camping near the pothole due to the potential for flash floods. The canyon widens after a couple of minutes and there are excellent campsites on slickrock benches. (2.0–2.5 hours.)

The canyon constricts into breathtaking narrows. There are small obstacles to overcome, minor route-finding challenges, and perhaps a short section or two of wading before you reach the crux narrows. (**Silver Falls Bench map.**)

The crux narrows

The crux narrows start at an eight-foot drop over a boulder into a pool. If the pool is shallow, the easiest path is to wade across it. Tall, strong climbers (basketball centers and the like) can chimney over the pool with a pack. To bypass the crux, hike back upcanyon for 100 yards and exit via a steep crack/slot (Class 3) to the left (LUC) (WSW). Scramble to the top of the Wingate—not all the way to the top of the Kayenta—and follow it downcanyon for several minutes until you are forced up the Kayenta to the top of a peninsula that runs west to east. Proceed to the east end of the peninsula and descend a steep chute (Class 3) into the canyon. The bottom of the chute is choked with wood.

To Horse Canyon

The remainder of Little Death Hollow holds no surprises. (**Red Breaks map.**) Short narrows and large pot-

Little Death Hollow.

holes can be easily skirted on ledges. There is good camping and plenty of water. After the canyon cuts through the Wingate and into the Kayenta, it intersects Horse Canyon. (2.0–4.0 hours.)

The exit route

Hike up Horse Canyon for ten minutes to the line cabin and fill up with water. It will take five to six hours to reach the next reliable water source in The Gulch. Up-canyon another ten minutes a constructed cattle trail exits the canyon to the left (NW). (The first part of the trail is shown one-half mile east-northeast of elevation 5678 on the **King Bench map**.) It is tricky to find. It goes up the first low spot in the Kayenta and you pass it while cutting corners on a track. Look for a large cairn ten feet above the canyon floor. The trail is easy to follow until it fades in an area of drift sand near the top of the hill. (1.5 hours.)

To The Gulch

Continue to follow the cattle trail as it leads initially northwest. In places it is six feet or more wide, revealing that it is still used. Before reaching Halfway Hollow the trail turns west, then drops into The Gulch (west of elevation 5322). (This is not the same cattle trail shown to the northwest of elevation 5685.) If you lose the cattle trail, do not panic! Simply continue northwest across King Bench. Halfway Hollow is easy to cross at any point and it is not difficult to find a route through the low Navajo walls that line The Gulch. This route even may be preferable to following the cattle trail into the Gulch: you can thus avoid much of the cattle-damaged and sullied canyon. (3.5–5.0 hours.)

Up The Gulch

There is always flowing water and there are fair campsites in The Gulch. As you hike upcanyon there may be some shallow wading. Cattle trails make the walking easy. There are many south-facing caves that were used by the Anasazi Indians. All of them have been looted by pot hunters. In two hours you pass a metal line shack. It will take another two hours to reach the trailhead. (4.0–5.0 hours.)

Option One. This route goes over Big Bown Bench into Silver Falls Creek, which it follows, and returns to Horse Canyon by way of Little Death Hollow. This route adds one day to the hike. Red Breaks, Silver Falls Bench, and Pioneer Mesa maps.

The exit route out of Horse Canyon

(Red Breaks map.) From the bottom of the cattle trail go up Horse Canyon for several minutes to a fence. To the right (E) is a constructed cattle trail going up a break in the Kayenta. Fill up with water before proceeding up the trail. The next reliable water source is in Silver Falls Creek, four to six hours away. Follow the cattle trail as it traverses east along Kayenta ledges and above the mouth of Little Death Hollow. A pump house and metal pipe are visible at the confluence. The pipe joins the trail at the interface between the Kayenta and Navajo. Follow the trail and pipe to a stock tank. You are now on Big Bown Bench. (0.5 hours.)

> **Historical note:** Big Bown Bench was named for Will Bown, a rancher who ran cattle and sheep in the area.

Across Big Bown Bench

You will notice a black rubber pipe going east from the stock tank. Follow it to the top of a hill, across a wide shallow valley, to the crest of another hill, and into a shallow canyon (shown one-quarter mile east of elevation 5626T on the **Silver Falls Bench map**). Drop into the canyon and follow it south. There are a couple of medium potholes in the canyon. A small side canyon comes in from the left (NE) just before a fall. There is a medium pothole above the fall. There is camping in the area. (1.0–1.5 hours.)

> **Digression:** The canyon below is a bit tricky to get into, but it has some rewarding attractions. (1.0 hour round-trip.)

Go southeast across a flat plain. The goal is to cross the top of the next side canyon that comes up from the Escalante River (shown to the west of elevation 5321T). This canyon has no water.

> **Rock-climber's note:** There is a route into this canyon which can be followed to the Escalante. Follow the left (E) rim of the canyon south for several hundred yards, past a large, level slickrock slab, to the only likely looking descent route. Downclimb a couple of short walls (Class 5.0, 15′); then zigzag down ledges into the canyon. Note the line of

Moqui steps near the top of the cliff. Follow the canyon down to the river.

To return, go up a Kayenta prow to the north (toward elevation 5217T) on a constructed cattle trail. This will take you to the top. Follow the rim of the canyon back to the start. (2.0–3.0 hours.)

Proceed south into an area of Navajo domes and intersect a wash going southwest (shown to the west of elevation 5356T). Follow it down a long stretch of shallow narrows until you are near the rim of a canyon. The farther down you go, the more likely you are to find small potholes. (0.5–1.0 hour.)

Exit the canyon to the left (LDC)(E) (discrepancies won't matter) and go southeast across broken ground to the rim of Silver Falls Creek. It is difficult to find the descent route, which starts at Cliff Spring (shown on the map).

Into Silver Falls Creek

Assuming you have intersected the rim of Silver Falls Creek south of the spring, follow the rim upcanyon. Stay near its edge. You are on Navajo slickrock, and the spring is at the interface between the Navajo and Kayenta. You will not be able to see the actual spring from the rim. First, find a Navajo prow with a vertical crack running up its middle on the far side of Silver Falls Creek. The prow is directly across the canyon from the spring. This will get you in the general area. Look for the bright white and green deposits that typically mark seeps on a wall, and also look for a round, silver water tank with a white-tipped fence that runs to it on a Kayenta bench. You may see a cattle trail on the bench.

Make your way down the Navajo on the upcanyon (N) side of the spring. Follow the cattle trail to the spring, which has a medium flow of water. There is no specific route down the cliffs into Silver Falls Creek. To get started, follow the cattle trail upcanyon (NE) for several minutes to a side canyon that goes southeast. (Do not make the mistake of continuing to follow the cattle trail northeast along Kayenta benches. Although there has been a lot of construction on the trail and it seems like it should go someplace important, it does not.) Follow the side canyon down to a short pour-off, then work down Kayenta ledges to the south. The final descent into the canyon is through the Wingate. If you should miss this route, do not fear. There are several other routes, including an old cattle trail, in this vicinity that will take you into the canyon. Some scouting may be necessary.

Silver Falls Creek has a medium flow of water where you join it. If the creekbed is dry, simply walk downcanyon. Water will appear shortly. (1.5–3.0 hours.)

> **Digression:** It is a short walk down to the Escalante and there is good camping near the river. (0.5 hours round-trip.)

Up Silver Falls Creek

Water now becomes a problem. There may be water for the first mile up Silver Falls Creek, but after that there is no reliable source until halfway down Little Death Hollow, six to eight hours away. Load up here.

In about twenty minutes you will reach the G.B. Hobbs inscription on a southwest-facing wall. A yellow plaque reads:

GEORGE BRIGHAM HOBBS

CHOPPED HIS NAME HERE ON HIS 24th BIRTHDAY FEB. 22nd 1883. HE WAS TAKING FOOD TO THE SAINTS AT MONTEZUMA, WAS ALONE AND HAD ONE HORSE AND MULE LOADED WITH SUPPLIES.

CAUGHT IN A STORM HE DID NOT THINK HE WOULD SURVIVE BUT AFTER FIVE DAYS IN SNOW HE WAS ABLE TO RESUME HIS JOURNEY.

ERECTED BY FAMILY JULY 5th 1957.

Upcanyon another thirty-five minutes is a huge, freestanding, abandoned meander to the right. Behind it is Emigrant Spring—which rarely has water. You enter the Chinle Formation near here. You can walk along portions of the old Charles Hall road that went down Harris Wash and up Silver Falls Creek.

Up the North Fork

The North Fork comes in from the left (NW) in forty-five minutes. Follow it. In about an hour and a half you will run into a thin layer of white rock (the Shinarump member of the Chinle) that contains medium springs and medium potholes. (The spring is shown, but is not labeled, one-quarter mile southwest of elevation 5585T on the **Pioneer Mesa map**.) (3.0–4.0 hours.)

To Little Death Hollow

A track passes the spring area on the left (LUC). Once you are above the spring area exit the road to the left (N). Your goal is to parallel the Wingate wall that is to the left (W) and follow it as it circles behind the Circle Cliffs and drops southwest into Little Death Hollow. Stay between the gray slickrock and the more convoluted red Chinle layers. At some point you will intersect an abandoned mining track. Follow it for a long distance until it peters out on a shoulder as you start to turn southwest. The canyon you follow into Little Death Hollow is between the Circle Cliffs to the south and a huge freestanding buttress (elevation 6377T) to the north. Join the standard route at the junction of the side canyon and Little Death Hollow near the Wingate boulders with petroglyphs. (2.0–3.0 hours.)

Wendy and Diz

The heat radiating from the slickrock was taking its toll as I struggled across the top of the Waterpocket Fold on a midsummer day many years ago. The glue that had held the soles on my boots had melted and I was finding that my quick fix—duct tape and parachute cord wrapped around the boots—was not up to the task. Diz, my Queensland red heeler, lagged far behind; her tongue hung out and her panting was palpable in the unbearable heat. We had started the day in East Moody Canyon. After finding a route up the Wingate walls of the Circle Cliffs, our goal was to traverse the Fold, locate the Baker Trail, and follow it into Stevens Canyon. Distances on the map often do not have a direct relationship to the time spent covering those spaces. There are too many intangibles: route-finding problems, cliffs to negotiate, and more ups and downs than the maps show. Diz and I were learning the hard way.

By late evening we had only made it to a spot marked "Cliff," the highest point on this part of the Waterpocket Fold. With just a couple of quarts of water left and unsure of exactly where to find the Baker Trail, I was worried. As night fell I set about making a dry camp. Diz disappeared. I knew she was searching for water; she had been looking all day. Diz had run up and down every drainage and had checked every pothole along our route. While I was eating dinner Diz came storming back into camp, prancing, dancing, and yelping. I immediately knew that she had found water, but I couldn't imagine where it could be in that maze of Navajo slickrock on the top of a ridge; it hadn't rained for a month or more.

Diz had been trained as a puppy not to drink out of potholes without my okay. Even as dehydrated as she was, she remembered the rule. Excited and thirsty, Diz made a nuisance of herself while I broke camp. She ran in circles and underfoot. I had a hard time following her as she raced down the cliffs to a magnificent reed-lined pothole overlooking the upper reaches of Stevens Canyon. Diz's find opened up the Waterpocket Fold country for me and made the Escalante South route possible.

Ten years later, Wendy Chase, her dog Solo, Diz, and I embarked on a sixteen-day trip into the Waterpocket Fold country. We wanted to explore the multitude of canyons and slots that fall from its crest. Philip Hyde, the inveterate desert explorer and photographer, had written, "Because of the steepness of the fold, many of its canyons may never be thoroughly explored." To Wendy and me, Hyde's pronouncement was like a gauntlet thrown down: we would explore the unexplored.

Wendy and I had been hiking and climbing together for years and had shared many adventures. Years of guiding in Montana had honed Wendy's backcountry skills, and a rigorous schedule of weight training, bouldering, and running kept her in shape while she held down a full-time job as a civil engineer in Boulder, Colorado. On weekends, Wendy teaches rock-climbing and mountaineering skills for the Colorado Mountain Club. She is also a member of Rocky Mountain Rescue. I was in good company.

We left the trailhead on Forty Mile Ridge with heavy packs. Hiking in November dictated that we bring winter-weight sleeping bags and lots of warm clothing. Wendy also carried food for her hundred-pound German shepherd. Solo had shredded her paws on a long climb down a chute lined with razor-sharp limestone and was in no condition to carry her own load.

I knew that the frustrations of big-city life and a demanding job had gotten to Wendy, because she set an unbelievably fast pace. At the Crack-in-the-Wall Wendy didn't stop to lower her pack over the edge; she simply walked down the top of a thin flake to the cliff dune below and zoomed down to Coyote Gulch. If we were to enjoy this trip, I knew I'd have to let Wendy set the pace for the first day and get the frustrations out of her system.

Wendy and Diz climbing out of the West Fork of Rock Canyon.

Mile after mile we raced; our enormous packs bounced on our backs and, even in the cold of winter, the sweat poured down.

I had planned to go up Stevens Canyon, follow the Baker Trail to the top of the Fold, and use Diz's pothole as a base camp while we explored the canyons to the east and west. But Wendy wasn't interested in the Baker Trail; she wanted a challenging route out of Stevens Canyon, and she found one a mile above the Baker Trail exit. Thin ledges, a difficult crack, and a steep, smooth slab with unnerving exposure led to the top of the Fold. A final pump brought us to Diz's pothole below Cliff just as it turned dark. Wendy had turned a three-day sojourn into a twelve-hour romp.

After exploring many side canyons, we hiked down the rim of Georges Camp Canyon to the edge of an escarpment far above the Escalante, hoping to find a route down. One of the axioms of canyoneering is that it is nearly impossible to find a route down cliffs while searching from the top. This rule held true as we looked for a sane passage. Giving up, we hiked back over the Waterpocket Fold to the mouth of Halls Creek, up the Red Slide, through the gap at Deer Point, and down East Moody Canyon to the Escalante.

We then hiked down the Escalante past Scorpion Gulch. Near the mouth of Georges Camp Canyon we noticed a cliff dune dropping through the escarpment on the right side of the river. Tired of wading and thrashing along the river, we ascended the dune, anticipating that it would take us out of the canyon. The dune led to a Kayenta ledge directly across the canyon from the cliffs near Georges Camp Canyon—the cliffs we had been trying to find a route down days before. With a good view of the cliffs, Wendy spotted a weakness in the Wingate above a long rubble slope and, after looking through binoculars, deemed that the route would go. It wasn't until a year later that Harvey Halpern, Bud Evans, and I found that the route Wendy had spied not only was easy, it was a bighorn sheep trail as well. This route to the Escalante became a part of the Escalante South hike.

Wendy and I continued our explorations. We found the old horse trail into Fools Canyon and the cattle trail out the other side. Many options were found for getting into Coyote Gulch, but our favorites were the Sleepy Hollow route and the climb down the prow of Jacob Hamblin Arch. The former was certainly more sensible and scenic; the latter was more invigorating and challenging.

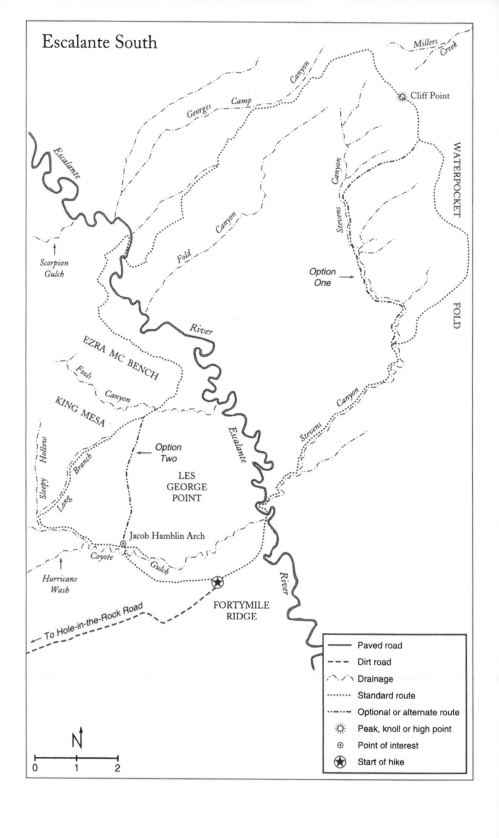

Escalante South

Millers Creek

Canyon

Georges Camp

☀ Cliff Point

WATERPOCKET FOLD

Escalante

Stevens Canyon

Scorpion Gulch

Fold Canyon

Option One

River

EZRA MC BENCH

Fools Canyon

KING MESA

Stevens Canyon

Sleepy Hollow

Long Branch

Option Two

LES GEORGE POINT

Escalante

⊙ Jacob Hamblin Arch

Coyote Gulch

Hurricane Wash

River

To Hole-in-the-Rock Road

★ FORTYMILE RIDGE

N

0   1   2

——————	Paved road
– – – –	Dirt road
⌒⌒⌒	Drainage
··········	Standard route
–·–·–·–	Optional or alternate route
☀	Peak, knoll or high point
⊙	Point of interest
★	Start of hike

The Escalante South

There is no royal road for the person who would explore the canyon's hidden secrets. Enthusiasm in unlimited quantities is a most needful qualification—enthusiasm in spite of discomfort, fatigue, and toil all to gain what might be a doubtful goal.

Ellsworth Kolb, 1914

General description:

This exceptional route takes you through the most remote area of the Escalante drainage, a region bounded by the Escalante River to the west and Lake Powell to the east. This area, the Waterpocket Fold, is a Navajo Sandstone wonderland that was named by Almon Thompson, a member of John Wesley Powell's second Colorado River expedition, for the many pockets of water he found among its slickrock draws, gullies, and canyons. The route combines the intimacy of canyon bottoms with the wide-open vistas of the cliff tops. Lush riparian habitats and vast expanses of slickrock merge into a symphony of colors and designs.

The first Indians to inhabit the area covered in this chapter were of the Desert Archaic Culture (6500 B.C. to 1500 B.C.). Only a few sites from this period have been discovered. Most of the relics, cave sites, and rock art panels you will see along the top of the Waterpocket Fold date back to the Anasazi Basketmaker II phase (1500 B.C. to A.D. 500). Sites along the Escalante River, Coyote Gulch, and lower Stevens Canyon are from the Pueblo II and Pueblo III periods (A.D. 900 to 1300).

In late 1879 and early 1880 Mormon pioneers constructed the Hole-in-the-Rock road in an incredibly difficult but successful effort to establish a route from the town of Escalante to the town of Bluff on the San Juan River. Two hundred thirty men, women, and children, along with 1,800 head of cattle and horses, made the arduous journey over a six-month period. Not a single life was lost.

The route of this hike starts at the end of Forty Mile Ridge, goes through the Crack-in-the-Wall, and descends a steep cliff dune to the confluence of Coyote Gulch and the Escalante River. From the Escalante the route goes up Stevens Canyon and exits via an old cattle trail that leads to the top of the Waterpocket Fold. The route then hopscotches down a succession of remote canyons back to the Escalante River. A cattle trail leads to the opposite rim of the Escalante. An exhilarating cross-country jaunt takes you in and out of Fools Canyon, into Coyote Gulch, and downcanyon to Jacob Hamblin Arch. You return to the trailhead by way of a steep slab dotted with Moqui steps.

Trip length:	Seven days minimum. Layover days, digressions, and options can add several more days to the length of the trip.
Elevation range:	3700′ to 6745′.
Recommended seasons:	March 1 to June 1 and September 15 to November 15. **Due to a lack of water along several sections of this hike, do not attempt it in hot weather.**
Maps:	7.5-series USGS topographic maps: King Mesa, Scorpion Gulch, Stevens Canyon North, and Stevens Canyon South. Metric maps: Escalante, Navajo Mountain, and Smokey Mountain. Two other maps, the Esclante Resource Area map and the Trails Illustrated map of the "Canyons of the Escalante," show the entire Escalante drainage, primary access roads, and mileage on the Hole-in-the-Rock road.
Skill level:	Most will find this a physically demanding route. There is difficult route-finding and Class-5.2 climbing. The leader must be familiar with belay techniques and be capable of leading the climbing sections without protection. There are many places with lots of exposure. There is a possibility of little water on some stretches depending on the season; but camping is always by water. There are short stretches of wading in shallow water.
Special equipment:	Wading shoes are essential. An eighty-foot climbing rope is adequate unless you choose one of the technical options. See the options at the end of the chapter for details.

Each hiker should have a minimum water capacity of two gallons.

Notes: This hike is in the Glen Canyon National Recreation Area. Hiking rules differ from those in Escalante lands administered by the BLM. You must register for the hike. This can be done at the ranger station in Escalante or at the trail register at the start of the hike. No fires are allowed. Dogs must be leashed. Group size is limited to twelve people.

All of Coyote Gulch and lower Stevens Canyon to the Grotto are often-visited areas and are showing signs of overuse. Although it is not a regulation, toilet paper should be carried out when in these areas. Do not camp in either area. Alternative campsites are mentioned in the text.

Escalante Outfitters, located in the middle of the town of Escalante, has all the maps for this route. They also carry backpacking equipment, freeze-dried food, and white gas. Showers and cabins are available. The Outfitters is open year-round. Their hours are 8:00 A.M. to 8:00 P.M., Monday through Saturday, and 1:00 P.M. to 6:00 P.M. on Sunday.

Administering agency: Glen Canyon National Recreation Area. P.O. Box 511, Escalante, Utah 84726. (801-826-4315) There is a combined BLM and Glen Canyon NRA ranger station on the west side of the town of Escalante. From November through April the ranger station is open Monday through Friday, 8:00 A.M. to 5:00 P.M. From May through October it is open seven days a week.

Land status: All of the lands covered in this hike are in the Glen Canyon National Recreation Area.

ROAD SECTION

The signed Hole-in-the-Rock road starts 4.5 miles southeast of the town of Escalante on Highway 12. It is a maintained dirt road to the signed Forty Mile Ridge junction. From there it is sandy in places and is suitable for high-clearance vehicles. In the dry season, sand traps can stop all but 4WD vehicles. The Hole-in-the-Rock road may be impassable when wet. There is camping along spur roads. Driving time from the town of Escalante is about two hours.

Drive down the Hole-in-the-Rock road for 36.5 miles to the "40 Mile Ridge 7 mi." sign. (If you come to Dance Hall Rock you have gone one mile too far.) Follow the track northeast toward Forty Mile Ridge. In 4.0 miles there is a large, round stock tank to the left on top of a rise. (The tank is east of elevation 4805 on the King Mesa map.) This may be as far as non-4WD vehicles can go. Continue for another 2.6 miles to a large parking area and trail register. You can camp at the trailhead. (The trailhead is located at a "Tee" in the track between elevations 4678 and 4625 on the **King Mesa map**.)

> **Alternate route:** If the road past the water tank is impassable, you have two choices: hike the road to the Forty Mile Ridge trailhead, or locate a route that starts at the water tank, and drops into Coyote Gulch. From the water tank look north-northeast and spot two squat domes. (The dome on the left is at elevation 4843.) Hike into the saddle between the domes, then go north down slickrock toward Coyote Gulch. As you descend, look for a huge, white, inverted Omega (Ω) near the top of the far wall of Coyote Gulch. It is the only white mark on the wall in this area. The descent route is a steep slab directly opposite the inverted Omega. You can see the entire route from the top of the cliff. The route down the slab is locally known as the Boy Scout route. Novice hikers may wish to be belayed (Class 4+, 120′). Note the Moqui steps part of the way down. This is also the exit route out of Coyote Gulch at the end of the hike.
>
> Hike down Coyote Gulch. There is lots of wading. It will take you four to five hours to reach the Escalante. Remember, plan your itinerary so you won't have to camp in Coyote Gulch.

Day One. 6.0 to 9.0 hours. King Mesa and Stevens Canyon South maps. There is water throughout the route.

Down Crack-in-the-Wall

(**King Mesa map** and **Map Twenty-two.**) After registering at the trailhead, follow a sandy track northeast down a hill and across a plain. When the track ends, follow a line of cairns north-northeast to the edge of an escarpment overlooking the Escalante River. (**Stevens Canyon South map.**) The cairns are regularly knocked over. If the route is not apparent, simply hike north-northeast across Navajo slickrock to the edge of the escarpment. Locate a long Navajo fin with a U-shaped gap extending northeast toward the river (shown on the map one-half mile east of elevation 4484T).

The Crack-in-the-Wall, a break through the Navajo, is 100 yards to the left (W) of the fin. After the first short drop it is simpler to lower your packs down a twenty-five-foot wall rather than try to squeeze them through the crack. Follow an established trail down a cliff dune to the left (W) side of a tower. Stevens Arch can be seen to the northeast.

> **Historical note:** Stevens Arch, the fifth-largest arch in canyon country, was named for Al Stevens, a rancher who ran cattle in the area. It has also been called Skyline Arch. Stories are told of daredevil pilots illegally flying through it.

> **Geology lesson:** Partway down the cliff dune the three formations of the Glen Canyon Group become visible to the northwest. The highest vertical cliffs are Navajo Sandstone. The red, ledge-forming cliffs below are the Kayenta Formation. The vertical cliffs at the bottom of the canyon are Wingate Sandstone. Note a large triangular-shaped talus slope with a trail running horizontally across it that drops from the base of the Navajo through the Kayenta. This trail is discussed in the alternate route below.

As you near Coyote Gulch, locate a trail that is thirty feet above the bottom of the canyon. (Do not hike down the streambed.) Follow the trail downcanyon, cross a steep slickrock slab (Class 3+), and descend an eight-foot wall to the canyon floor. (1.5–2.5 hours.)

To Stevens Canyon

Wade down Coyote Gulch for ten minutes to its confluence with the Escalante River. Continue wading, up the

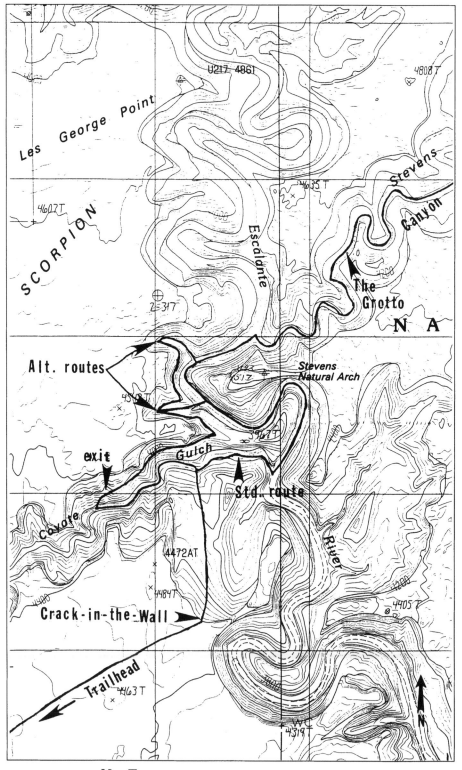

Map Twenty-two

David Bone and Larry Breed in the Crack-in-the-Wall.

sand-bottomed Escalante River to Stevens Canyon, the first canyon to the right (E). (1.0–1.5 hours.)

> **Alternate route:** This route must be used if the water level in Lake Powell is high. Hike up Coyote Gulch for about fifteen minutes to the first area of campsites on the right (LUC). They are ten feet above the canyon floor and are shaded by huge cottonwoods. A large spring flows from a wall 100 yards further upstream on the right.

From the downcanyon end of the campsite, locate an established and cairned trail zigzagging up Kayenta ledges to the north. The trail turns northeast and traverses the aforementioned talus slope to a saddle on a peninsula across from Stevens Arch (at elevation 3967T). The trail turns northwest. Follow it for ten minutes to the first side canyon dropping to the Escalante (SE) (shown one-eighth mile east of elevation 4542T). You intersect the canyon before passing the fin containing Stevens Arch. There is a small spring at the top of the canyon. Follow a cairned route down the canyon to the river.

Should the lake be particularly full, continue traversing upcanyon to the next side canyon. This canyon is hard to descend (Class 4) and has an almost impenetrable barrier of vegetation at its mouth. Wade up the Escalante to Stevens Canyon. (Add 1.0 hour.)

Up lower Stevens Canyon

Do not remove your wading shoes yet. The first mile of Stevens Canyon has a half-dozen or more crossings and is a bit of a thrash. Pass the first deep pool on the left (LUC) by climbing a log and a row of Moqui-style steps (Class 5.0, 20', belay and hand up or haul packs). Go by the second pool on the right. Hikers have built a pyramid of rocks to help ease the difficulty (Class 4, 12'). The wading comes to an end after a couple of hundred yards. (1.0–1.5 hours.)

In fifteen minutes a trail goes up a slippery, poison-ivy-choked rockslide. Before negotiating the hill, visit the Grotto fifty yards to the left (LUC)(W). It is an exquisite alcove with a pool at its base, topped with a unique natural bridge. Above the rockslide the canyon is intermittently dry.

The route continues up Stevens Canyon. It passes a nice side canyon (shown to the north of elevation 4819T) coming in from the right (E). There are occasional poison-ivy patches, willow and tamarisk thickets, and other small obstacles to overcome. The bushwhacking ends in an area of wonderfully fluted slickrock and artistically varnished Wingate walls. At the end of the slickrock the canyon is blocked by a pour-off (north-northwest of elevation 4883T). Note the Moqui steps on the right-hand wall. They lead to a short dead-end slot (Class 5.8, 25'). Happily, there is no more poison ivy for the remainder of the trip. There are good campsites in the area. (2.5–3.5 hours.)

> **Water:** There is a large pool at the base of the pour-off. Except in the dry season, there is usually water running down the fluted slickrock.

Day Two. 4.0 to 6.0 hours. Stevens Canyon South and Stevens Canyon North maps. There are large springs along the route and large potholes at the end of the day.

Up middle Stevens Canyon

(Stevens Canyon South map.) To continue up Stevens Canyon, backtrack from the pour-off for several hundred yards to the first rubble heap leading up the Wingate wall to the left (LDC)(E). Scramble up it, follow a wide ledge downcanyon for 100 yards, and ascend a steep slickrock ramp northeast to the top of the Wingate (Class 3+). Hike upcanyon (NE) on the top of the Wingate and along Kayenta ledges. Stay near the rim of the canyon. At the first corner, note the rockslide coming down from the Navajo wall to the right. This huge section of rock fell in the summer of 1991.

Continue hiking on top of the Wingate for almost two hours.

> **Digression:** The first steep slope dropping through the Wingate into the canyon bottom provides access to many medium potholes and short slots. There is excellent slickrock camping in the area. However, do not continue up the floor of the canyon, since there is no easy exit out its top.

The trail descends the second steep slope back into the bottom of the canyon above a fall just as the Wingate wall to the right nearly disappears. Note the small natural bridge and large pothole at the top of the fall. (2.5–3.5 hours.)

In thirty minutes the canyon divides three ways (south-southwest of elevation 5087T). Watch carefully for this junction—it is somewhat hard to see. Turn left (W), stay-

Stevens Canyon.

ing in the main canyon. Pass a large pothole on either side. The canyon bottom is intermittently sand- and slick-rock-floored. It has a seasonal flow of water and contains a string of inviting pools. In fifty minutes the canyon narrows for 100 yards. There are two large elongated potholes surrounded by slickrock—a perfect place for a break, and a dip if there is running water. It is important to recognize this area, because the exit out of the canyon is a short way up and is hard to locate.

Nine minutes upcanyon from the elongated potholes the canyon turns right, from northwest to northeast. The Wingate wall to the right (E) is short and broken. At the far side of the corner a short section of constructed cattle trail is barely visible twenty-five feet above the ground. This is the exit route. **(Map Twenty-three.)** (If you go too far upcanyon you will see a long, straight stretch lined with grasses, willows, and cottonwoods that is marked as a spring on the map). There is camping in the area. (1.5–2.5 hours.)

Water: There is usually water in the elongated potholes. The spring area upcanyon from the cattle trail exit generates a large flow of water.

Option: See "Option One—Alternate Day Two" for details

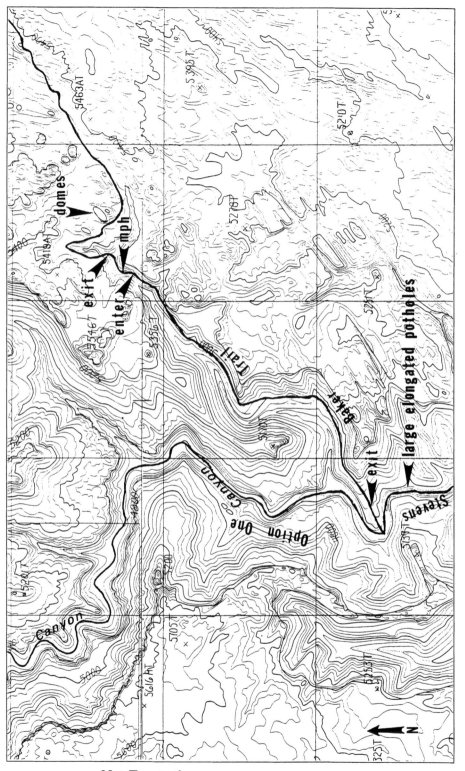

Map Twenty-three

on a challenging exit near the top of Stevens Canyon. This exit is for experienced canyoneers and rock climbers only.

Day Three. 8.0 to 11.5 hours. Stevens Canyon South and Stevens Canyon North maps. There are medium potholes at the end of the first hour, otherwise this is a dry day. There are large potholes at the end of the day.

> **Warning:** This is an exceptionally long and tiring day with a lot of elevation gain, route-finding problems, and no water. Make sure you are prepared. A jump-start the night before or a start at the crack of dawn is essential.

Exit Stevens Canyon

(**Stevens Canyon South map.**) Exit the canyon via the cattle trail to the northeast. The constructed part is short and ends on Wingate slickrock. Follow the top of the Wingate northeast, staying near the rim of the canyon. Below you is the spring area with its numerous huge cottonwoods.

> **Historical note:** The cattle trail is locally known as the Baker Trail. It was named for a rancher who used to run cattle in the upper portions of Stevens Canyon and on the Waterpocket Fold.

Within ten minutes you will intersect and follow the Wingate rim of a side canyon coming in from the east (shown to the east of elevation 5170T). Follow the serpentine course of the side canyon on top of undulating waves of slickrock for a half hour until the Wingate tapers and a trail drops to the bottom of the canyon. Hike up the canyon. There are medium potholes in the canyon and, if the potholes are full, this area could be used for camping on Day Two.

(**Stevens Canyon North map.**) Minutes after entering the canyon, a very small side canyon comes in on the left (NW) at the end of the Wingate. One minute past the small side canyon there is another small canyon to the left (N) with two cottonwoods and a pinyon pine near its mouth (shown one-eighth mile south-southeast of elevation 5419AT.) A large cairn is immediately downstream in front of a large juniper tree. You will exit the canyon here. (If you go too far, the canyon ends in a fall.)

Exit the side canyon

Surmount a seven-foot wall (Class 4) behind the aforementioned pinyon pine and continue up the side canyon for a minute or so until it is possible to exit it by scrambling up steep ledges to the left (W) to the top of the Kayenta. There is a section of the old cattle trail near the top. Follow the rim of the side canyon north, head it, and return to the rim of the main canyon. Continue upcanyon. In several more minutes, after passing a series of Navajo domes that are to the left (LUC), drop into the shallow upper part of the main canyon. Do not head it; instead, go northeast up the sand-floored canyon.

The canyon divides almost immediately. Stay to the right (NNE) (immediately north of the "5" in elevation 5463AT). In twelve minutes the canyon divides again, just before a split pinnacle. Stay to the right (E). Several minutes later the canyon divides again. Stay to the right (NE) for several paces; then follow a trail up a hill to the right (E). At the top of the hill, you will find yourself in a shallow drainage for a hundred yards. The trail exits the drainage to the left (N) up a hillside and then quickly enters another shallow drainage going east-northeast. The drainage goes generally northeast to the crest of the Waterpocket Fold. This section is confusing. If you miss the trail, do not panic! Simply wend your way northeast up draws and around domes until you are on the crest of the Fold. (You will end up on the top of the Fold between elevations 5642T and 5658T.) (3.0–4.5 hours.)

> **Historical note:** As you walk along you will notice depressed areas containing innumerable flakes of chert and jasper. These are called lithic scatters and are evidence of the Anasazi Indians who roamed the Waterpocket Fold during the Basketmaker phase of their culture (1500 B.C. to A.D. 750). The scatters consist of chips left over when the Indians flaked larger pieces of rock into spear points and scrapers.

> **Digression:** For those wishing to drop down to Lake Pow-

ell, go east across the Fold. The Baker Trail continues down to the lake. (2.5–4.0 hours.)

To Cliff

Follow the crest of the Fold generally north. This looks straightforward, but there are several false summits and a couple of shallow canyons to cross. After recent rains, there may be water in scattered pothole locations along the Navajo sections. "Cliff" (labeled on the map as Cliff at elevation 6745) is the highest point on this section of the Fold. There are several labeled bench marks on its Navajo summit. (5.0–7.0 hours.)

The views from the top are incredible:

East: Bullfrog Basin and marina on Lake Powell.
North-northeast: The Little Rockies. The closest peak is Mt. Ellsworth (8,253′); the most distant is Mt. Holmes (7,998′).
Northeast: Below you are the cliffs of Halls Creek.
North: The Henry Mountains. In the foreground is Mt. Pennell (11,132′); in the background is Mt. Ellen (11,506′). Millers Creek Canyon is below you.
Northwest: Boulder Mountain.
West: The Aquarius Plateau.
Southwest: The Kaiparowits Plateau.
South-southeast: The rounded summit of Navajo Mountain (10,346′).
Southeast: In the far distance, the long butte with a tower in the middle is in Monument Valley.

Water: From Cliff look southwest into the bowl of upper Stevens Canyon. Note a large freestanding tower with a smaller tower on its right side down in the bowl (elevation 6361T). Walk directly toward the right side of the larger tower (SW). You are searching for a large shallow pothole with cattails in it that is 150 yards inland from the rim. A huge, cattail-choked pothole can be found 200 yards to the east-southeast of the shallow pothole if you go over a rise and drop into a deep depression. (Both water sources are a quarter mile west-northwest of the spring shown on the map.) It may take some scouting to find the potholes. Remember that bighorn sheep and deer depend on these potholes for water. Camp at least 300 feet from them and do not visit them at night.

Day Four. 4.5 to 7.5 hours with the Essential Digression. Stevens Canyon North map. There are no reliable springs along the route. There are several large potholes mentioned in the text. Fill up with water whenever you are able.

Finding the descent canyon
   (**Stevens Canyon North map.**) The descent canyon is hard to locate. Follow directions and your map carefully. From Cliff look north into the square-topped head of Millers Creek Canyon. Make your way north along the top of the Fold until you are even with the northwest end of Millers Creek Canyon. (**Map Twenty-four.**) Go northwest, following the crest of the Fold, for another twenty minutes. You will pass the head of a white, shallow, Navajo slickrock–lined canyon. This is the descent canyon. (It starts at elevation 6601AT and goes southwest. It is one-third mile west of elevation 6641T.) (1.5–2.5 hours.)

> **Essential Digression:** To make certain you descend the correct canyon, continue past the top of the descent canyon for about ten minutes until you can see the red Wingate walls of East Moody Canyon to the west-northwest. There are no other red-walled canyons in the vicinity. Backtrack to the descent canyon. **Do not try to find the descent canyon without first locating East Moody Canyon.** There are a couple of similar-looking Navajo-lined side canyons that feed into the descent canyon, but they contain impassable falls. (0.5 hours round-trip.)

> **Historical note:** East Moody Canyon was not named for its temperament but for John Moody, a rancher who ran cattle in the area.

The descent canyon
   Go southwest down the shallow sand-floored canyon for twenty-five minutes to a fall. Pass it on the right (LDC). There are a couple of small, easily negotiated falls before you reach a string of large potholes that are 200 yards above an impassable fall. There is camping in the area. (1.0–1.5 hours.)
   To pass the fall, backtrack for a couple of hundred yards to the top pothole and ascend a slope to the left

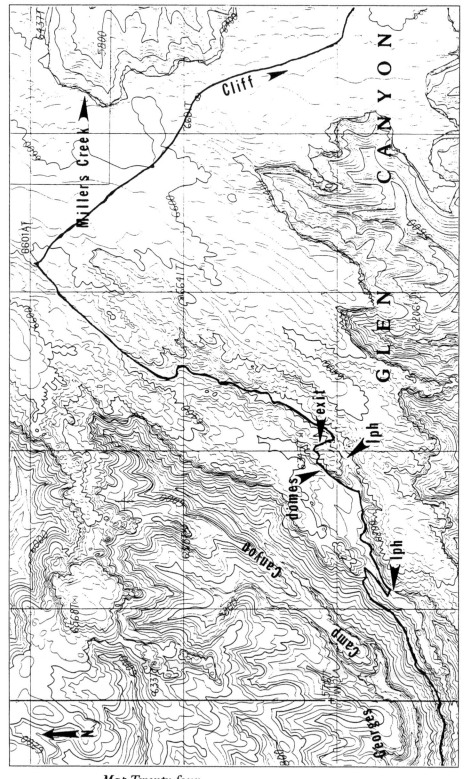

Map Twenty-four

(LUC)(W) to the foot of a Navajo ridge (elevation 6345T). Follow the base of the ridge upcanyon until you are between the second and third domes. The first two domes have rounded tops; the third is more pointed. Scramble up between the domes and negotiate a short wall behind a juniper (Class 4) to a saddle.

From the saddle look south at a ridge that drops into a shallow canyon to the north. Make your way to the ridge, using the branches of a pinyon pine to help you ascend a short slab (Class 4). Descend very steep slickrock into the canyon (Class 4). A short distance downcanyon there is another drop. Pass it via a less-than-vertical crack on the right (Class 4+, 40′, belay and lower packs). The Navajo walls and domes below are sublime.

At the next impassable fall, exit the canyon up a short hillside to the right (NW) to a long, thin saddle with fantastic views and excellent camping. The deep, impressive canyon to the north is (LKA) Georges Camp Canyon. (1.5–3.0 hours.)

> **Water:** There is a large reed-filled pothole immediately before the fall.

Day Five. 5.0 to 8.5 hours. Stevens Canyon North and Scorpion Gulch maps. There are several large potholes mentioned in the text.

Canyon hopping to the Escalante

(Stevens Canyon North map.) The route gets complicated. Pay close attention to the text and to your maps. Proceed to the north end of the saddle until you come against a Navajo dome. Descend a chute to the west. Traverse southwest, following a bighorn sheep trail along Kayenta ledges. (Do not drop to the top of the Wingate.) Scramble up to the first notch in the Navajo ridge to the left (S). **(Map Twenty-five.)** The notch has a dome in its middle. (The notch is one-half mile east-northeast of elevation 5816T.) (1.0–1.5 hours.)

From the notch, look south across the canyon to another notch in the Navajo. Cross the canyon and hike into that notch. (The notch is one-eighth mile northeast of elevation 5673T.)

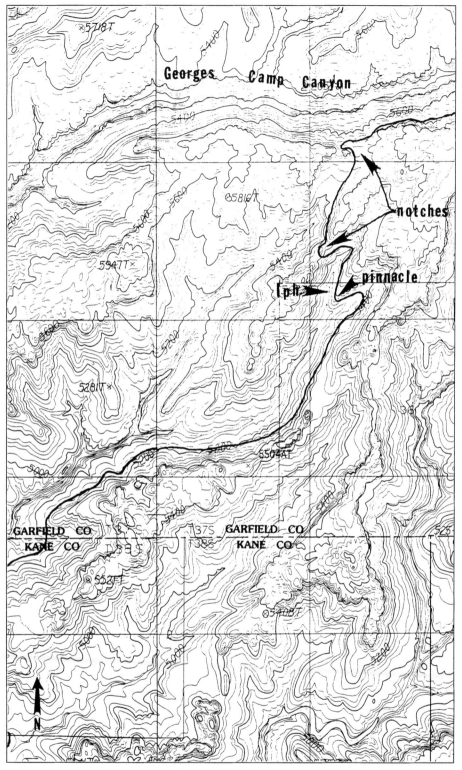

Map Twenty-five

From the notch, look south into the next canyon. You will see two canyons coming together in a "Y," with a twenty-foot pinnacle at their junction. Descend a steep Kayenta wall to the south. The route is tricky—it has loose rock and may take some scouting (Class 4, lower packs). Descend the canyon on its left (LDC) side until you are below the pinnacle at the "Y." Head the short canyon that forms the left arm of the "Y." There are large potholes in both canyons. Hike southeast to the top of the Wingate. There is excellent slickrock camping in the area. (1.0–1.5 hours.)

Follow the top of the Wingate along the south edge of the canyon for an hour. **(Scorpion Gulch map.)** Locate a large, dominant, freestanding tower (elevation 5405T) on the opposite (W) side of the canyon. Several minutes past the tower you will be forced to the head of a short side canyon. From its top, look up to the east. The Navajo cliffs that have been to your left (S) end in a final tower that has two windows. Exit the canyon here by hiking to the top of the Kayenta ridge to the southeast (one-quarter mile east-northeast of elevation 5164T).

Descend Kayenta ledges south to the rim of another canyon (shown one-quarter mile south of elevation 5164T). This canyon contains several large potholes; however, it is a bit troublesome to get into. There is good camping in the area. (1.0–1.5 hours.)

Head the canyon and follow its south rim west-southwest for ten minutes to a notch to the south between the Navajo wall and a prominent dome (elevation 5441T, the one nearest the Escalante River). **(Map Twenty-six.)** Hike through the notch and descend Kayenta ledges south into a Wingate-lined drainage. Follow it west until you are on the rim of the Escalante River Canyon. Go southeast over a short ridge to the rim of a small canyon, head it, and return to the rim of the Escalante.

Descend to the Escalante

The route-finding becomes even more tricky. Looking southwest, you will see a broken promontory of rock and a long talus slope extending northeast to southwest toward the Escalante. (The promontory is shown one-quarter mile east of elevation 5095T and immediately south of

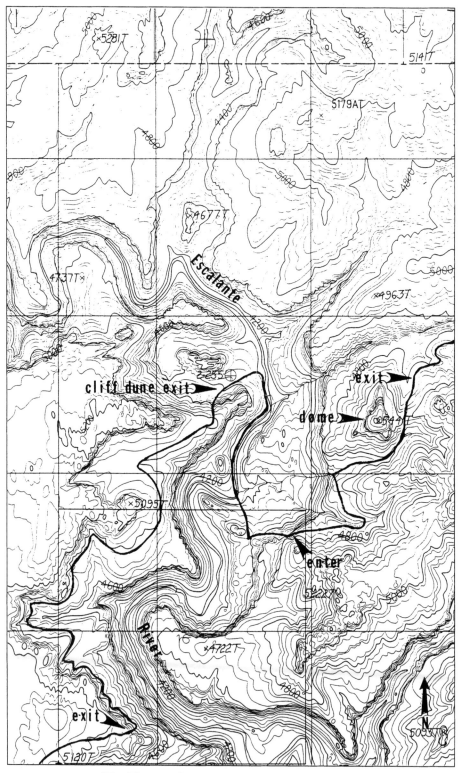

Map Twenty-six

a marked 4200-foot contour line.) Traverse southwest along the face of the escarpment, going up Kayenta ledges only as needed in order to make further progress. Look for a bighorn trail. After going about seventy-five feet above the Wingate, you will be forced onto a three- to five-foot-wide ledge. The ledge cuts horizontally across the face of the cliff for 200 yards and ends at the top of a slope leading out to the promontory. It is best to scout the route without a pack. Search carefully, as the ledge looks like it peters out in several places. (If you go too high, you will find yourself on a wide ledge below a Navajo cliff and you will walk above the desired ledge system.)

> **Warning:** The ledge is not technically difficult (Class 3+), but it is very scary. Belays can be utilized. Packs should be lowered in one obvious place to assure that hikers aren't accidentally launched off the ledge.

Once you are on the promontory, descend a steep slope to the north and go down a shallow drainage to the Escalante. There is good camping on a broad sandy beach across the river. The beach is below the Chinle Formation. This is the first time the Chinle has appeared on the standard route. (2.0–4.0 hours.)

> **Water:** The Escalante always contains water. Cattle are run throughout the canyon; therefore, treat the water with extra care.

Day Six. 5.5 to 7.5 hours. Scorpion Gulch and King Mesa maps. There is no reliable water until the end of the day.

Exit the Escalante

(**Scorpion Gulch map.**) Hike north up the west side of the Escalante River (no wading) for twenty minutes to the base of a cliff dune that drops east through the Kayenta, Wingate, and Chinle formations. This is the only sand dune in the vicinity. (The cliff dune is south of an abandoned meander shown on the map as 2-223.) Ascend the dune to the west. Near the top, find a cattle trail

Lee Motor and Larry Breed on the bighorn sheep trail down to the Escalante River.

(LKA the Scorpion Horse Trail) going up the Kayenta to the south. Note the brush fence at the top. (1.0–1.5 hours.)

Follow the cattle trail generally south on a wide Kayenta bench; cross a couple of small canyons and head others. After forty-five minutes the trail heads the back of a larger canyon that has two distinct alcoves. Past this, the trail crosses a wide plain in front of another side canyon. The Kayenta ledge narrows considerably and you will see a Navajo dome near the end of a ridge on the right (LDC). This is the first break in the Navajo wall and it is the exit route. (If you go too far, the trail turns sharply south at a corner and goes toward the back of a long side canyon or bay.) (The ridge is shown one-quarter mile east-northeast of elevation 5120T and just northwest of a marked 4600-foot contour line.)

Climb up the Kayenta (Class 4, haul packs) and locate a pour-off between the Navajo wall and the Navajo dome. Ascend a crack on the right side of the pour-off (Class 5.2, 10′ of climbing, 25′ of exposure, belay and haul packs). Follow the drainage up for 100 yards until it divides. Go west up the prow between drainages and work southwest until you are between two squat, elongated, Carmel-topped domes. The dome to the left is flat-topped; the dome to the right is rounded. Without a pack, hike to the top of the dome to the left (E). (1.5–2.0 hours.)

Into Fools Canyon

(King Mesa map.) Walk to the southeast end of the dome and look east-southeast. In front of you is a deep, wide side canyon or bay. The tallest, bare-topped, some-what-pointed dome is marked elevation 5165 on the map. To the right of it, a couple of miles in the background, is a flat, Carmel-topped dome (elevation 5170). This dome is your goal. It is easiest to pass the initial jumble of domes at the head of the long side canyon or bay by pass-ing around its back side and dropping on steep slickrock into a canyon. (This is shown as a small drainage west of elevations 5110 and 5058.) There is a large pothole a quarter mile down this canyon in a section of narrows. Hike up the canyon back to the rim.

Once you are past the domes, stay within 200 to 300 yards of the rim of the Escalante, hiking on pleasant slick-rock and across sandy plains until you reach the top of the aforementioned destination dome (elevation 5170). **(Map Twenty-seven.)** (1.5–2.0 hours)

From the top of the dome, go south-southeast across a juniper-studded plain and down steepening slickrock to a bowl with a long, prominent, southwest-running rib on its west side. (The bowl is immediately west of elevation 5010.) You will see a long peninsula of red Navajo Sand-stone jutting southwest far into Fools Canyon on the south side of the bowl (shown one-third mile west of ele-vation 4827 and immediately north of a 4400-foot con-tour line). Make your way to the top of the rib and descend it, traveling southwest into the bowl. Note the steps hacked into the rock to facilitate getting horses up and down. Walk to the south end of the bowl. A wide side canyon drops into Fools Canyon, with the peninsula on the left (LDC)(E). To the right of center is a rubble heap that goes down the Navajo and into the canyon.

Do not drop to the bottom of the canyon; instead, fol-low a game trail down the right side of the canyon on a Kayenta bench until the Navajo ridge on the right ends at a prow. From the end of the prow, descend to the bottom of a canyon to the right (NW) by first hiking upcanyon

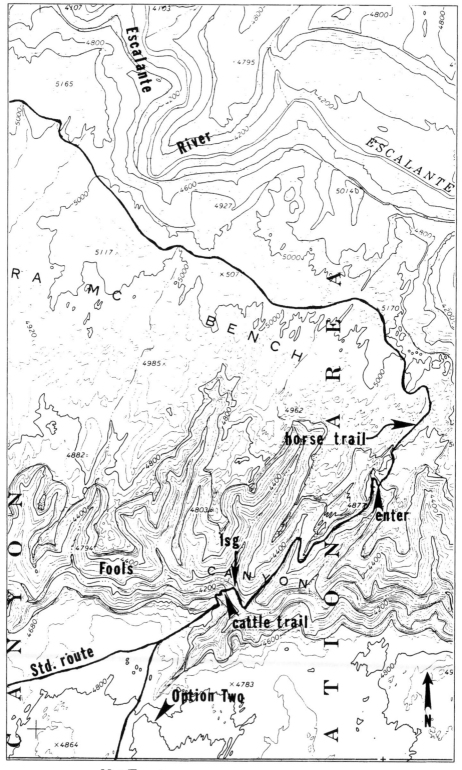

Map Twenty-seven

Tony Somkin and friends on the constructed horse trail into Fools Canyon.

for two hundred yards, then zigzagging down steep ledges to the floor of the canyon (Class 4-). Follow the canyon into Fools Canyon.

Thrash your way up Fools Canyon through thick vegetation for ten minutes until you are above a huge deep pool—the ultimate swim hole, if there is running water. There is camping in the area (1.5–2.0 hours.)

Water: There is always water in the pool and perennial springs are downcanyon.

Day Seven. 7.0 to 9.0 hours. King Mesa map. There are large potholes along the route, but you may have to spend some time looking for them.

Exit Fools Canyon

(**King Mesa map.**) Hike upcanyon from the swimming hole for 200 yards to a trail coming in on the left (SW). (The trail starts to the north of a side canyon that is shown on the map to the north of elevation 4783.) This is an old constructed cattle trail, and it is easy to follow as it makes its way up the Kayenta and Navajo.

The trail disappears near the top. Hike southwest to the rim of the canyon. (1.0 hour.)

> **Option:** There are now two route alternatives to consider. The first is technically easier and is presented below as the standard route. It crosses King Mesa and drops into Coyote Gulch above its confluence with Hurricane Wash. The second alternative, presented as Option Two (see page _), has difficult route-finding and several rock-climbing sections that entail rope work. This route is for accomplished rock climbers only. The route goes below the southern end of King Mesa and enters Coyote Gulch via a stimulating climb down the face of Jacob Hamblin Arch.

Into Coyote Gulch

From the rim, you will be able to see King Mesa, a long flat-topped Navajo ridge, to the west-southwest. On its left (S) side is a rounded slickrock hill (elevation 5026). The mesa itself is split by a pass (shown at elevation 5020) near its south end. The pass may not be apparent until you get closer to it. Make your way west-southwest over, around, and through a maze of domes and washes to the pass. (1.0–1.5 hours.)

Descend a canyon that starts at the pass and goes south. As the canyon deepens and narrows, stay as close to its left (LDC) rim as possible. This slot canyon is called the Long Branch of Sleepy Hollow (AN). (**Map Twenty-eight.**)

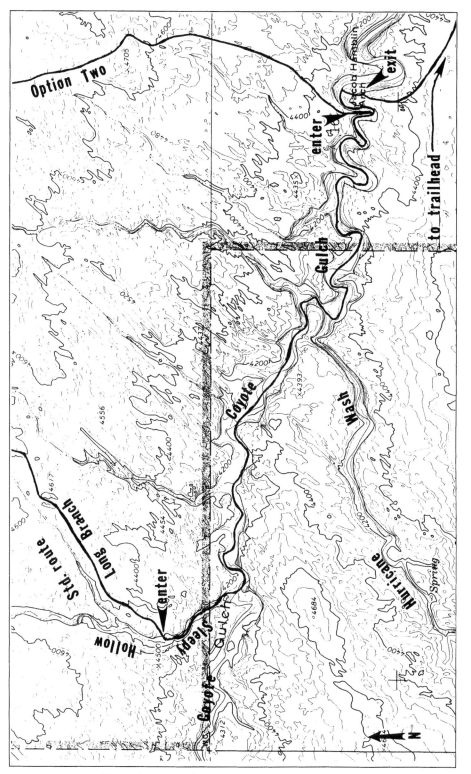

Map Twenty-eight

Note: There are many large potholes in the canyon and there is great camping along the slickrock. Remember, Coyote Gulch is being heavily impacted by campers. Do not camp in Coyote Gulch.

The narrows end above a wide canyon (LKA Sleepy Hollow) that has towering walls and a profusion of cottonwoods along its floor. Simply continue along the rim for another couple of minutes until you can descend moderate slickrock southwest into Sleepy Hollow.

Digression: Sleepy Hollow has a perennial flow of water. Though choked with Russian thistle and other vegetation, the upper reaches of the canyon are especially beautiful. (1.0–1.5 hours round-trip.)

Hike down Sleepy Hollow to Coyote Gulch. (1.5–2.0 hours.)

Down Coyote Gulch

The farther down Coyote Gulch you go, the higher the walls rise. A riparian habitat develops as the stream becomes larger. Cottonwoods line the canyon. By now you will be constantly wading back and forth across the stream. Hurricane Wash, a narrow defile, enters from the west in about forty-five minutes. The canyon narrows even more in the vicinity of Jacob Hamblin Arch. (2.0–2.5 hours.)

Historical note: Jacob Hamblin was sent to southern Utah in the 1850s by Brigham Young. He was the first Mormon missionary to visit the area and befriend the local Indians. Hamblin was also a scout and an explorer—he proved invaluable to John Wesley Powell during the latter's Colorado River adventures. The arch was originally named Lobo Arch by early ranchers.

Exit Coyote Gulch

To exit Coyote Gulch, hike past Jacob Hamblin Arch. Just as the arch disappears from view, ascend a steep trail to the right (LDC) to a sandy platform forty feet above the creek. Climb horizontally across a slickrock slab toward the arch (W) for twenty-five yards, then climb a steep slab (Class 4+, 120′, some may want a belay), using Moqui steps in places, to the top of the cliff. From the top of the Navajo, cut east-northeast cross-country back to the trailhead. (1.5–2.0 hours.)

> **Digression:** It takes six to eight hours to dayhike down Coyote Gulch to the Escalante River and back. It is certainly worth seeing Coyote Natural Bridge and visiting the waterfalls and pools in the lower end of the canyon. An alternative is to backpack down the canyon and exit via Crack-in-the-Wall. Plan on five to seven hours to the trailhead. Plan your itinerary so you won't have to camp in Coyote Gulch.

Option One—Alternate Day Two. This route continues up Stevens Canyon and exits via an exciting climb to the top of the Waterpocket Fold. 7.5 to 10.5 hard hours. (The time starts at the campsite at the end of Day One.) Stevens Canyon South and Stevens Canyon North maps. There are large springs for most of the day and large potholes at the end of the day.

> **Warning:** This option is for rock climbers only: the exit out the top of Stevens Canyon has two pitches of moderate Class-5 climbing. A ninety-foot climbing rope is essential.

Upper Stevens Canyon
(Stevens Canyon South map and **Map Twenty-three.)** Continue up Stevens Canyon. Seven minutes from the Baker Trail exit you will pass a side canyon coming in from the right (NE), its mouth partially obscured by huge cottonwoods. Stay in the main canyon to the left (NNW) (west of elevation 5170T). The next section of canyon contains abundant vegetation and numerous large springs. In another thirty minutes **(Stevens Canyon North map)** a boulder-filled side canyon comes in from the right (NE) (shown to the west of elevation 5546T). Stay in the main canyon to the left (NW). In another ten minutes a side canyon comes in on the right (N) (shown to the east of elevation 5201T). There is a mine claim written on a boulder at its mouth. Follow the main canyon to the left (W). The vegetation and springs end soon. This may be the last nonpothole water available until the end of Day Five.

In another fifty-five minutes two canyons enter from the right: the first from the northeast, the second from the north. (They are shown to the south-southeast of elevation 5277T.) The Chinle Formation is visible at this junction.

Continue up the main canyon to the west for another thirty-five minutes to a short boulder-choked canyon entering from the right (NE) (shown to the southwest of elevation 5637T). This side canyon is easy to miss. You will exit the main canyon here. **(Map Twenty-nine.)** There is camping in the area, but the preferred campsite is another forty-five minutes away on top of the Wingate. (2.5–3.5 hours.)

> **Water:** Water is sometimes available from a small seep next to a cottonwood 100 yards up Stevens Canyon. To locate a large spring, go twenty minutes up Stevens Canyon to the first side canyon on the right (NE). Go up this side canyon for fifteen minutes to the spring area.

Exit Stevens Canyon

From the mouth of the small side canyon that is the exit route (not the canyon with the spring), go up Stevens Canyon for 100 yards, then work your way north-northeast up a steep slope through a short band of cliffs to the top of the Wingate. There are several possibilities (Class 3+). Once on top, traverse upcanyon along the Wingate, parallel to the main canyon.

In ten minutes you will intersect a side canyon going northeast. Follow its rim. In thirty minutes you will be forced away from the canyon by a narrow side canyon. At its head is an arch in a Navajo wall. There is excellent camping on a peninsula on the far side of the narrow side canyon. (1.0 hour.)

> **Water:** The upper part of the narrow side canyon below the arch contains large potholes.

Option One—Alternate Day Three. 4.5 to 7.5 hours. Stevens Canyon North map. There is no reliable water until the end of the day.

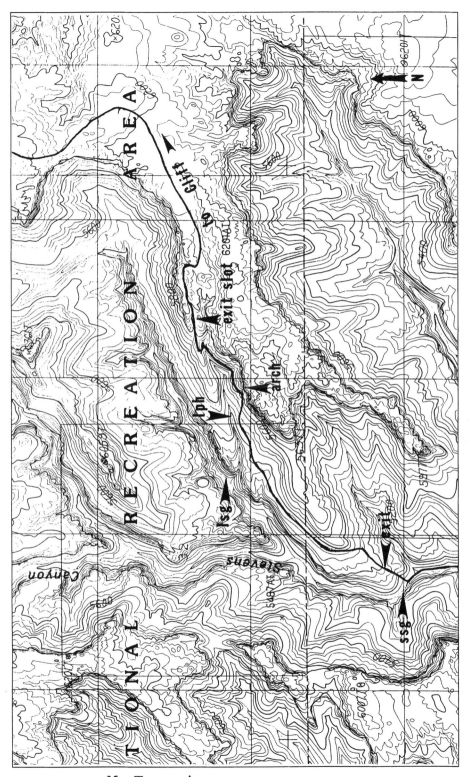

Map Twenty-nine

To the top of the Waterpocket Fold

(Stevens Canyon North map.) From the top of the narrow side canyon go east up the Kayenta (Class 4-) until you are near the base of the Navajo. Traverse north on ledges and pass directly under the arch. Ten minutes past the arch is a shady alcove with a small hanging garden. Immediately past the alcove, go up a small canyon coming in from the east-northeast. It narrows and steepens. Climb up a chimney to a small stance (Class 5.4, 18', belay and haul packs), then continue up a chimney (Class 5.1, 25', belay and haul packs). Both pitches have loose rock. (1.5–3.0 hours.)

The route becomes impossible to describe because there is a maze of domes, cliffs, small canyons, and many dead ends. As a rule go east. Stay on top of the Navajo, not in the canyon bottoms, until you are forced down into a canyon that goes east (shown immediately north of elevation 6201AT). Follow it up to the top of the Waterpocket Fold. (You will be between elevations 6205T and 6540T on the map.) (1.0–1.5 hours.)

Work your way north along the top of the Fold through a labyrinth of Navajo domes, across several shallow washes and canyons, and over an amazing variety of slickrock. This section is not easy. Stay as close to the ridgeline as possible until you are on the highest point on the Waterpocket Fold. This is called Cliff on the map. There are several bench marks on the top. See the end of Day Three—standard route—for information on camping and water. (2.0–3.0 hours.)

Option Two. This route enters Coyote Gulch by way of a climb down Jacob Hamblin Arch. 5.0 to 8.0 hours from Fools Canyon to the trailhead. King Mesa map. There is no reliable water until Coyote Gulch.

> **Warning:** This option is for rock climbers only. Although climbers can be belayed on the climb down the prow of Jacob Hamblin Arch, the last person will be at risk; there is no protection possible. There is Class-5.2 climbing. A 120-foot climbing rope is essential.

Into Coyote Gulch

(King Mesa map.) From the rim of Fools Canyon, hike south across slickrock and sand, passing between the southeast end of King Mesa and Rock (elevation 4961), a large Navajo dome to the left (E).

From the top of a ridge past these two points, locate a small flat-topped dome in the distance to the south (elevation 4843), silhouetted against the Kaiparowits Plateau. There is a less-distinct, elongated dome to its right. These domes are on the far side of Coyote Gulch near the round water tank mentioned in the Road Section.

Into Coyote Gulch

Proceed south across fantastic slickrock toward the right side of the elongated dome to the edge of Coyote Gulch. **(Map Twenty-eight.)**

> **Water:** With some searching you should be able to find large potholes along the route. There is great camping on the slickrock. Remember, Coyote Gulch has been heavily impacted by campers. Do not camp in Coyote Gulch.

If ali has gone well, Jacob Hamblin Arch will be visible down the canyon. If it is not, scout the rim until you find it. You can see it from both up and down the canyon. (Jacob Hamblin Arch is labeled on the map.) Once you are on the rim, it is easy to locate yourself on the map because of the sinuous nature of Coyote Gulch. Do make sure that you accurately locate the arch. There are many steep prows that project into the canyon and end in impassable drops.

Walk to the top of the arch and scramble and climb down (S) its prow into Coyote Gulch (Class 5.2, 120', belay and lower packs. This can be done in either one or two pitches). It is advisable to scout the route first. (2.5–5.0 hours, depending on how long it takes to locate the arch and belay hikers down it.)

See Day Seven for directions on exiting Coyote Gulch and returning to the trailhead.

I turn away with regret, feeling freshly molted. Down in the canyon I grew a little, understood a little more, perceived even more, and in so doing split the carapace of time and place I commonly wear. Split it, wriggled out of it, left it there, a stiff and empty shell to be blown away by a canyon wind. The new skin was extra-sensitive, and so I perceived the canyon about me with new eyes, more sensitive touch, emotions closer to the surface, and I walked protective of this as yet unhardened integument.

Ann Zwinger, 1978

BIBLIOGRAPHY

Abbey, Edward, and Philip Hyde. *Slickrock—The Canyon Country of Southeast Utah.* San Francisco: Sierra Club Books, 1971.

Abbey, Edward. *The Monkey Wrench Gang.* Philadelphia: J.B. Lippincott Co., 1975.

Allen, Steve. *Canyoneering: The San Rafael Swell.* Salt Lake City: University of Utah Press, 1992.

Austin, Mary. *Land of Little Rain.* Boston: Houghton, Mifflin and Co., 1903.

Baars, Donald L. *Canyonlands Country: Geology of Canyonlands and Arches National Parks.* Revised Edition. Salt Lake City: University of Utah Press, 1993.

Baars, Donald L., and C. M. Molenaar. *Geology of Canyonlands and Cataract Canyon.* Durango, Colorado: Four Corners Geological Society, 1971.

Backer, Howard, M.D. "Field Water Disinfection." *Journal of the American Medical Association* 259 (June 3, 1988): 3185.

Baker, Pearl. *Robbers Roost Recollections.* Logan, Utah: Utah State University Press, 1991.

___. *The Wild Bunch at Robbers Roost.* New York: Abelard-Schuman, 1965.

Berger, Bruce. *The Telling Distance.* Portland, Oregon: Breitenbush Books, Inc., 1990.

Breed, Jack. "Roaming the West's Fantastic Four Corners." *National Geographic* 101 (June 1952): 705–42.

Brower, David, ed. *Wilderness: America's Living Heritage.* San Francisco: Sierra Club Books, 1961.

Bureau of Land Management. *Utah Statewide Wilderness Study Report. Volumes IIA and IIB—Summary Analysis of Study Area Recommendations.* United States Department of the Interior, Bureau of Land Management, 1991.

Coughlan, Robert. "Vernon Pick's $10 Million Ordeal." *Life* 37 (Nov. 1, 1954): 112–28.

Crampton, C. Gregory. *Standing Up Country: The Canyon Lands of Utah and Arizona.* New York: Alfred A. Knopf, Inc., 1964.

Dellenbaugh, Frederick S. *The Romance of the Colorado River*. Chicago: Rio Grande Press, 1904.

___. *A Canyon Voyage*. New Haven: Yale University Press, 1962.

Finken, Dee Anne. *A History of the San Rafael Swell*. Price, Utah: Resources Development Internship Program, Bureau of Land Management, Moab District Office, 1977.

Forgey, William W., M.D. *Wilderness Medicine*. Merrillville, Indiana: ICS Books, Inc., 1987.

Frazier, N.A., et al. "Production and Processing of U.S. Tar Sands: An Environmental Assessment." Cincinnati, Ohio: Industrial Environmental Research Lab, 1976.

Frost, Kent. *My Canyonlands*. New York City: Abelard-Schuman, 1971.

Gregory, Herbert E., ed. "Diary of Almon Harris Thompson." *Utah Historical Quarterly* 7 (Spring 1939): 3–138.

_____. "Journal of Stephen Vandiver Jones." *Utah Historical Quarterly* 16 (Spring 1948): 11–174.

Henderson, Randall. *Sun, Sand and Solitude*. Los Angeles: Westernlore Press, 1968.

Kelly, John R., ed. *Social Benefits of Outdoor Recreation*. Urbana-Champaign: University of Illinois, 1981.

Kirk, Ruth. *Desert: The American Southwest*. Boston: Houghton Mifflin Co., 1973.

Kolb, Ellsworth L. *Through the Grand Canyon from Wyoming to Mexico*. New York: Macmillan Co., 1937.

Kolb, Ellsworth L., and Emery Kolb. "Experiences in the Grand Canyon." *National Geographic* 26 (August 1914): 99–184.

Lambert, Neal. "Al Scorup—Cattleman of the Canyons." *Utah Historical Quarterly* 32 (Summer 1964): 301–20.

L'Amour, Louis. *Dark Canyon*. New York: Bantam Books, 1963.

Loope, David B., et al. "Abandonment of the Name Elephant Canyon Formation in Southern Utah." *The Mountain Geologist* 27 (October 1990): 119–30.

McClenahan, Owen. *Utah's Scenic San Rafael*. Castle Dale, Utah: n.p., 1986.

Miller, David E. *Hole-in-the-Rock*. Salt Lake City: University of Utah Press, 1959.

Powell, John Wesley. *The Exploration of the Colorado River and Its Canyons*. New York: Dover Publications, Inc., 1961.

Regens, James L. *Energy and the Western United States*. New York: Praeger Publishers, and CBS Educational and Professional Publishing, 1982.

Ringholz, Raye C. *Uranium Frenzy*. New York: W.W. Norton and Co., 1989. Paperback reprint, Albuquerque: University of New Mexico Press, 1991.

Schneeberger, Jon. "Escalante Canyon—Wilderness at the Crossroads." *National Geographic* 142 (August 1972): 270–84.

Utah Wilderness Coalition. *Wilderness at the Edge*. Salt Lake City: Utah Wilderness Coalition, 1990.

Van Cott, John W. *Utah Place Names*. Salt Lake City: University of Utah Press, 1990.

Van Dyke, John C. *The Desert*. Salt Lake City: Peregrine Smith, Inc., 1987.

Wilkerson, James A. *Medicine for Mountaineering*. Third Edition. Seattle: The Mountaineers, 1990.

Zwinger, Ann. *Wind in the Rock*. Tucson: University of Arizona Press, 1978.